NOBILITY AND NEWCOMERS
IN RENAISSANCE IRELAND

Nobility and Newcomers in Renaissance Ireland

Thomas Herron

Brendan Kane

Folger Shakespeare Library
Washington, DC
2013

This volume has been published in conjunction with the exhibition *Nobility and Newcomers in Renaissance Ireland* presented at the Folger Shakespeare Library, Washington, DC, from January 19 through May 19, 2013.

Michael Witmore, *Director*

Stephen Enniss, *Eric Weinmann Librarian*

Thomas Herron and Brendan Kane, *Curators*

Caryn Lazzuri, *Exhibitions Manager*

Eric Brownell, *Exhibitions Consultant*

This catalog has been funded by Furthermore: a program of the J. M. Kaplan Fund, and by The Winton and Carolyn Blount Exhibition Fund of the Folger Shakespeare Library.

All photographs by Julie Ainsworth unless otherwise noted.

Cover image sources: See pages 25, 56, 64, and 88. Above: Detail from *Civitates Orbis Terrarum*, Map of Galway, 1618? (see page 108).

Printed in the United States on acid-free paper by Penmor Lithographers; Smythsewn and bound by Acme Bookbinding.

Design and typography by Bruce Kennett.

Furthermore:
a program of the J. M. Kaplan Fund

CONTENTS

FOREWORD

THE HISTORY OF RELATIONS between Britain and Ireland has at times emphasized borders more than crossings. That history has sometimes seemed to be preoccupied with notions of identity as defined by family, province, or nation rather than identity that is dynamic and still emerging. This exhibition challenges these fixed ideas from two directions: through an examination of nobility in Renaissance Ireland and from the perspective of newcomers to this ongoing and progressive story.

Brendan Kane and Thomas Herron, co-curators of *Nobility and Newcomers in Renaissance Ireland,* challenge us to think beyond the Pale, to think differently about cultural and political exchange between Ireland and Britain in the sixteenth and seventeenth centuries, and to think differently about belonging and the often hybrid nature of identity in the period.

This is the first exhibition on Ireland to be held at the Folger Shakespeare Library, though the collection has long supported the study of early-modern Anglo-Irish relations. While the Folger holds one of the finest collections in North America of early English printed books and manuscripts, it also documents the powerful historical forces shaping a wider early-modern world. In fact, the Folger contains an extensive historical record for the study of Ireland in the sixteenth and seventeenth centuries, and this accompanying catalog offers only a glimpse of a small number of the books, maps, manuscripts, and works of art that illuminate this history.

We may think of globalization as a modern phenomenon, but *Nobility and Newcomers in Renaissance Ireland* reminds us that the history of Britain and Ireland has from Tudor times to the present always been interconnected. It reminds us of the rich history of the peoples of these two islands and indeed of a broader Atlantic world still in the making.

This exhibition has been conceived by its co-curators but made possible by the support of many people. It is our great pleasure to share it with the public and to share as well this companion publication.

Stephen Enniss
Eric Weinmann Librarian
Folger Shakespeare Library

acknowledgments

This exhibit has been a joy to assemble in spite of a hurricane, an earthquake, and a presidential campaign. We would like to thank the Folger staff, in particular Caryn Lazzuri for her enthusiasm, openness to ideas, constant help, and advice. Head Librarian Stephen Enniss has been wonderfully supportive and helpful, including with this catalog. We thank Eric Brownell and Emily Robinson for their efforts plumbing the library's cold depths for materials and tracking down images in other archives.

Steven Galbraith, former curator at the Folger, first approached us in 2009 at the "Elizabeth I and Ireland" conference in Storrs, Connecticut, with the idea of curating an exhibit on Ireland, which we eagerly agreed to do. He has been an inspiration for our work ever since.

Thanks to Bruce Kennett for creating a gorgeous catalog out of a mass of texts and images, and to Doris J. Troy for ennobling our prose.

Many people suggested materials to include and made loans possible that have informed this catalog. These include Hiram Morgan, Valerie McGowan-Doyle, Eva Griffith, John Bradley, Catherine McKenna, Tómas Ó Cathasaigh, Neil Buttimer, Hilary Bogert-Winkler, and Michael Potterton. Of particular note, Jane Fenlon arranged for the plaster image of Elizabeth, and Pádraig Ó Macháin supplied facsimiles of Irish texts courtesy of the Dublin Institute for Advanced Studies' "Irish Script On Screen" (ISOS) project. Without the latter, there would have been very little Irish-language presence in the exhibition and catalog, and thus the story could not have been told. We are fortunate to have such a generous and supportive network of scholars to rely upon for help and advice—responsibility for all errors, of course, lies with us.

Finally, we thank our families. Curating this exhibit has taken us away from them more than we ever thought it would. For their love, patience and support, we are eternally grateful.

Go raibh míle maith agaibh go léir!

Thomas Herron and Brendan Kane
Thanksgiving Day 2012
Greenville, North Carolina, and Storrs, Connecticut

FIGURE 1   Queen Elizabeth II listens to harpist Siobhan Armstrong during the royal visit to Ireland, Trinity College Dublin, May 17, 2011. Photo by John Stillwell–Pool/Getty Images.

INTRODUCTION

NOBILITY AND NEWCOMERS have long shaped Ireland's affairs and culture, no more so than in the early-modern period. Ireland at this time was a country of invasions, continuity, and change; of ideas, languages, art, and literature; of armies, settlers, merchants, and magnificent lords. Early-modern nobility and newcomers to Ireland came from an astonishing range of places and social backgrounds—the nobility were sometimes newcomers themselves. Both groups turned Ireland into a melting pot of cultures and a place of significant opportunity and creativity, amid great turmoil and destruction.

The recent royal visit of Queen Elizabeth II of Great Britain to the Republic of Ireland, May 17–20, 2011 (fig. 1), was extraordinary for several reasons. For one, it demonstrated that the enduring strains in the relationship between the two countries, which prevented the Queen from visiting until the forty-ninth year of her reign, are healing. It was the first visit by a reigning British monarch since her grandfather George V toured in 1911, when the country was still part of Great Britain. By visiting the island as a reigning English monarch, Elizabeth followed her forebears Edward VII, Victoria, George IV, William III ("of Orange"), James II, Richard II, John, and Henry II.

Second, as this chronicle of royal names attests, Elizabeth's visit brought renewed attention to the continuing and long-lasting ties between England's nobility and the island, Ireland, that it had ruled for more than eight hundred years. (Indeed, a sizable portion of the island remains part of Great Britain today.) Elizabeth's visit was a sensational event, with many critics and supporters. The publicity surrounding it is an indication that the people of both islands remain fascinated by the continuing role played by English nobility in Irish affairs. There is another side of the coin, however: What role did the Irish nobility play in English affairs?

Nobility and Newcomers in Renaissance Ireland tells part of that story, as it relates to early-modern Ireland.[1] The rich collection of the Folger Shakespeare Library sheds light on this cultural exchange between the two islands, and between Ireland and continental Europe as well. Ireland in the period was a truly international place. *Nobility and Newcomers in Renaissance Ireland* provides a window onto the varied landscape of Ireland's political elite, its English and Irish nobility and the people who strove to join their ranks in a time of great crisis and opportunity. Until recently, historians tended to bypass questions of noble identity in Ireland and often ignored how it changed and adapted during the period of the northern European Renaissance (c. 1500–1700), arguably Ireland's most dramatic and traumatic period after the Anglo-Norman conquest (1180s) and before the Great Famine (c. 1845–50). This exhibition tells the story of that tumult and change, of destruction, adaptation, and survival.

The Folger Library has long promoted research on early-modern Ireland. Among American institutions, the Folger took the lead when in 1966 it published D. B. Quinn's highly influential monograph, *The Elizabethans and the Irish* (see fig. 2). The present catalog is meant as an interdisciplinary follow-up to Quinn's work and accompanies the first exhibition on Ireland to appear at the Folger.

By studying the world of the Irish nobility, we examine not only the upper class but also the crosscurrents of culture that affected all

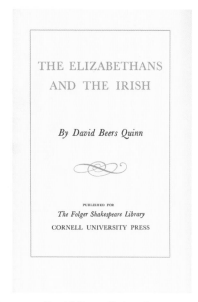

FIGURE 2 David Beers Quinn (1909–2002).
The Elizabethans and the Irish (Ithaca, NY: The Folger Library and
Cornell University Press, 1966), title page. Folger Shelf Mark DZ937 .Q5.

of Irish society. We also study the nobility partly out of necessity: They produced much of the only material evidence (in addition to letters and state papers, there are works of art, architecture, and literature) that remains from those years.

Nor were the nobility in early-modern Ireland entirely Irish: They were profoundly international in both blood and culture. They were shaped, first and foremost, by a longstanding hybridization with English, Scottish, and Welsh families—that is, with their near neighbors. They had deep and enduring links with the Continent as well: Ireland is a large island in the North Atlantic, and most of its coastal cities were founded by the Vikings, who were raiders and traders. Towns, rural settlement, and international trade prospered thereafter, in the later Middle Ages. Eventually, the country participated in the great burgeoning of arts and letters that was the Renaissance.

The purpose of this exhibition is therefore twofold: to demonstrate

Irish culture and nobility and to emphasize the country's connections to both England and the wider world. "No man is an island," wrote the poet John Donne, and, paradoxically, no island is either.

Ireland today is a republic that comprises twenty-six counties. Six more counties, all in Ulster, form Northern Ireland, and are part of Great Britain under a constitutional monarchy.

Ireland in the early-modern period was unified as a kingdom under the English, then British, crown, and consisted of three main social groupings: Gaelic (or native) Irish, Old English, and New English. The Gaelic Irish were direct descendants of the families *in situ* before the Anglo-Norman conquest, in the later twelfth century CE. Most remained Catholic in the early-modern period, despite the pressures of the Protestant Reformation (which never got far in Irish society), and they spoke Irish as their first language. Many adhered to ancient Irish legal principles, courts, titles, and churches, separate from those of the English system.

The Old English were the early-modern descendants of the original Anglo-Norman conquerors. They too remained Catholic, for the most part, after the Reformation, and many spoke Irish in addition to English (and in some cases Latin and French) as their primary languages. They proudly considered themselves to be English and often adhered to English law, although many were deeply hybridized in their culture: in some cases, "degenerating" or becoming "more Irish than the Irish themselves" (to quote contemporary commentators), long before the sixteenth century. They were especially strong in the towns and their hinterlands, including the Pale, the area around Dublin ruled by the crown.

The New English were mostly soldiers, settlers, and administrators who arrived in the late sixteenth and seventeenth centuries as part of a renewed wave of English conquest, colonization, and administrative reform. They were usually Protestant, in line with the Tudor and Stuart

FIGURE 3 Portumna Castle. Photo courtesy of the National Monument Service, Department of Arts, Heritage, and the Gaeltacht.

monarchs (except Queen Mary), and thus brought the Reformation with them.

Each social group had its commoners and elites, including nobility. For example, the Protestant first Earl of Essex, who died in Ireland in 1576 after attempting to colonize the Ards in Ulster, and who held on to Irish lands that passed to his descendants, could be seen as a "New English" nobleman, although he and his heir, the second Earl, spent most of their lives at home on their main estates in England. Among the most prominent Old English noblemen were the earls of Kildare, Ormond, and Desmond, and among the most prominent Gaelic Irish noblemen were the earls of Tyrone and Thomond, et al.

Many of us are aware of a lost "Gaelic" past infused with ideas of ancient nobility. Tara, for example, the name of Ireland's ancient ceremonial center of kingship, is also the name of Scarlett O'Hara's plantation home in Margaret Mitchell's *Gone With the Wind* (1936). It is an idealized place of southern domestic calm and landed wealth disrupted by civil war.[2] Many places associated with the Irish nobility in the early-modern period can still be found and visited, some of them as romantic and war-torn as Mitchell's Tara.[3] Some are in ruins and some have recently been restored. Portumna Castle (fig. 3), County Galway, former seat of the Old English Earl of Clanricard, has had its shell restored by the Office of Public Works and its interior made into exhibit space.[4] Bunratty Castle, County Clare, former seat of the Earl of Thomond, has a delightful folk museum, and visitors can enjoy a

xii

"medieval" feast in the castle itself. The ruins of Maynooth Castle, County Kildare, former seat of the Old English Earl of Kildare, now hold an exhibit on its history. Blarney Castle (fig. 4), County Cork, where once dined the MacCarthy lords of Muskerry, descendants of the high kings of Munster and now famous for a kissing stone, is a highly profitable ruin in private hands.[5] In the north, Dunluce Castle, County Antrim, seat of the MacDonnell earls of Antrim, has recently been excavated (fig. 5).[6] Many of the ancient inauguration sites of the Gaelic Irish kings can also be seen and have been studied extensively.[7]

Despite their constant and evolving traces in today's landscape, many of the noble families of Ireland have been absorbed into other lineages, declined, or died out. Yet some found a way to survive, and indeed thrive, during the early-modern period. Some flourished by engaging intimately with the English (and other) nobility, just as the English have always profited by engaging with the Irish. This trend, one of adaptation, change, and success involving both countries, runs contrary to a popular historical narrative that stresses only the decline and "death of the Gael" after the Flight of the Earls in 1607 (see pages 77–79).

Although battered, the nobility in Ireland (both Old English and native Irish) were not utterly ruined by this great event. Surprisingly, some members even joined the parliamentary, antiroyalist cause during the War of the Three Kingdoms and subsequent Cromwellian conquest of Ireland (1649–53): Such was the shameful case of Murrough O'Brien, Earl of Inchiquin, who in 1647 burned the Rock of Cashel and everyone in it. The earl switched sides in 1648, however, and fought for the Royalist cause. Irish loyalties in the period were no more fixed than were English ones.

FIGURE 4 View of Blarney Castle ruin.
Photo used with kind permission from Blarney Castle.

FIGURE 5 Dunluce Castle, County Antrim. Photo by Stuart Caie.

The Folger Shakespeare Library contains not only many historical documents, but also numerous literary ones related to the topic of nobility in Ireland. Famous writers such as Shakespeare, Edmund Spenser, James Shirley, and John Milton addressed Irish issues, and many had noble patrons who became intimately involved with Ireland. So did lesser-known poets such as Barnabe Googe and Lodowick Bryskett. Some wrote more generally about issues of nobility from their bases in Ireland: When Spenser praises Queen Elizabeth I as Gloriana in *The Faerie Queene,* for example, he is celebrating her imperial reach everywhere, not just in north County Cork, where he lived. At the same time, his humble shepherd's criticism of the vanities of her court had universal application.

Some Irish-language poets—Eochaidh Ó hEodhusa, for example—wrote works despite (or because of) the problems besetting their patronage networks among the native Irish and Old English elites; in some cases, these poets branched out to new genres and new patrons, even to some in England. The Irish histories of writers and antiquarians such as Richard Stanyhurst, James Ware, and James Ussher also flour-

ished in this period (see pages 19, 97, and 103, respectively). They re-defined Ireland's past and future according to her noble houses and those of appointed English lords deputy, whose patronage they sought.

The extent of the historical interaction between English and Irish nobles on both islands is astonishing. Long before the Renaissance or the Anglo-Norman invasion, for example, St. Patrick (d. 461?) was a Briton abducted from Wales and enslaved in Ireland who escaped back to Britain and then returned to Ireland to convert Irish kings and their followers (or so the story goes). Ireland's patron saint "belongs," therefore, to both islands.

Across centuries, Ireland has been typecast as the victim of English colonial aggression, hence of subjugation by English lords, but conquest went two ways: As Shakespeare well knew (see page 3), Ireland contributed to invasions of England on more than one occasion, and Ireland played an important part in the fifteenth-century Wars of the Roses as a base of support for enemies of and claimants to the English throne. A thousand years earlier, in the late-Roman/early-medieval period, North and South Wales held significant Irish colonies, as did Cornwall and Devon.[8] Scotland is named after the Irish, the Scoti, who subjugated the Picts and the Britons, perhaps in the late fifth century, and helped to convert them to Christianity. Iona, a cradle of early Irish monasticism, located in the Western Isles of Scotland, was founded by the Irish monk Colum Cille (c. 521–97), a.k.a. St. Columba, who came from a noble branch of the O'Donnells in Ulster. Columba is notable because he was a war-faring aristocrat who joined and therefore helped to bolster the nascent Christian church in Ireland and Scotland. Columba's history was written c. 700 in Latin by the monk St. Adom-nán, and again, c. 1532, in early-modern Irish by the Donegal chieftain Manus O'Donnell. O'Donnell, who claimed kinship with Columba, wrote in the vernacular and according to other principles of Renaissance historiography. He resituated the story of early Christianity in the north of Ireland and Scotland by placing it within the context of his

XIII

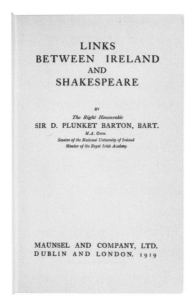

FIGURE 6 Sir Dunbar Plunket Barton (1853–1937).
Links Between Ireland and Shakespeare (Dublin and London: Maunsel and Company, 1919), title page. Folger Shelf Mark PR3069.I7 B3.

own noble family and traditions, in a modern mode of writing based on international, Renaissance models.[9]

Shakespeare knew of Columba's mission, perhaps from Raphael Holinshed's *Chronicles* (published in 1577). Iona is mentioned in *Macbeth* as Colmekill, the final resting place of Duncan, the last Scottish king to be buried there: "Colmekill, / The sacred store-house of his predecessors / And guardian of their bones" (*Macbeth* 2.4.31–4). As noted by Sir Dunbar Plunket Barton in his groundbreaking *Links Between Ireland and Shakespeare* (1919), published in London and Dublin (fig. 6), all of the principal characters in *Macbeth* have names of Irish origin (Macbeth, from the Irish *mac beatha,* means "son of life," for example; a related phrase is *uisce beatha,* "water of life," which gives us *whiskey*). King James VI of Scotland, later James I of England, likewise traced his roots to King Fergus, a legendary Irishman from prehistory (see page 69).

Like King James, the early-modern Irish nobility could be highly cosmopolitan. Although an island, Ireland was always in contact with the wider world. Continental connections go back at least as far as the Bronze Age (c. 2500–500 BCE). It is thought that in this period, Celtic settlers-cum-invaders from the European mainland, progenitors of the old Irish kings, brought with them the Gaelic language, as well as more-advanced weaponry, thereby transplanting (or absorbing) the people they found there who spoke a different language. During the Iron Age (c. 500 BCE–500 CE), the Middle Ages, and the Renaissance, the Continent continued to influence Ireland's noble culture(s) and her art, architecture, and letters, not only via the English who settled there (see pages 45–49), but also through centuries of trade and contact by way of Ireland's many harbors and port towns (see page 48). The Irish lords them-selves, like their priests, took many opportunities to travel to the Continent, often in exile but sometimes returning (see chapter 10).

It must be emphasized, then, that interaction between Irish and English cultures in the early-modern period was not simply one of lop-sided colonial domination. The Irish people and their language long suffered under English rule, without a doubt.[10] Despite the violence, however, and active discrimination by a burgeoning Protestant elite minority (which created, for example, Ireland's penal laws against the Catholic majority, laws fully abolished only in the 1830s) along with the near-destruction of the Irish language (a process greatly accelerated in the nineteenth and twentieth centuries), each country influenced the other in peaceful terms as well. The nobility were a ready conduit of "higher" learning and culture between Ireland and her sister island. It is surprising to learn, for instance, that an Irish earl (Clanricard) of Old English extraction (Burke) married the widow both of the second Earl of Essex and of Sir Philip Sidney (Frances Walsingham) and owned a modern estate in Kent, England (Somerhill), described in Gaelic poetry by a visiting Irish bard. The poet complains that the earl's attentions have wandered too far abroad.[11] Another Irish poet, Piarais Feiritéir, in Irish extols the beauty of an English noblewoman, Meg Russell, who lived in London in the 1630s. A century earlier, Henry Howard, Earl of Surrey, had famously praised the Irish aristocrat Elizabeth Fitzgerald, daughter of the Earl of Kildare, as "the Fair Geraldine" at the Tudor court (see page 25).

This exhibition focuses not only on the established nobility, but also on the newcomers who were patronized by them and strove to become ennobled in the sixteenth and seventeenth centuries. These New English "adventurers," as they were sometimes called, some of them soldiers, some administrators, some settlers, some investors, some writers, succeeded beyond their wildest dreams in creating posterity for themselves, in land or literature and sometimes both. Early-modern Ireland was a land of opportunity for down-and-out aristocrats as well as for those who wanted to fashion themselves into nobility.

Their major colonial projects, including plantations, sowed seeds of the British Empire at home and farther abroad. While Sir Walter Raleigh was funding and promoting the "Lost Colony" in the Outer Banks of North Carolina in the late sixteenth century (a colony that likely contained Irishmen, including a Butler), he and many other Englishmen (and a few Irish, Welsh, Cornish, and Scots) were plotting the Munster Plantation in the southwest of Ireland (see page 41). The Munster Plantation's major benefactor in the long term was not, ironically, Raleigh himself but instead Richard Boyle, later first Earl of Cork and the father of an illustrious line of scientists, writers, and administrators of the British realms. Boyle went west and arrived in Munster in the 1580s as a young man of modest means. By 1620 he was one of the wealthiest men in Europe, with a notoriously extravagant family tomb in St. Patrick's Cathedral, Dublin (see page 87): a remarkable success story if ever there was one. Social climbing was a hallmark of early-modern Ireland, which was also a laboratory for models of colonial exploitation.

Despite this history of parvenus, social climbers, and opportunistic scoundrels, many Irish Americans tend to think of Irish nobility not in modern terms but rather in terms of their own families' long-lost roots amid the Celtic clans. From their point of view, the noble names they carry (MacCarthy, O'Brien, O'Toole, O'Neill, O'Byrne) originate in a romantic, because also lost, ancient past. Not all Americans realize that they may be connected to Irish nobility should their names come from Anglo-Norman stock instead. Among such noble families who arrived in Ireland in the twelfth century are Fitzgeralds, Berminghams, Butlers, Burkes, Laceys, and Barrys. Moreover, if an American descends from a sixteenth-century newcomer to Ireland, such as a Smith, Coote, Bingham, King, or Boyle, he or she might also have a claim to an Irish title somewhere, sometime. In other words, some Americans may descend from Irish nobility because they are, in fact, English.

It is fair to say that most ancestors of Irish Americans came to America's shores impoverished. But the "Irish" nobility crossed oceans in the early-modern period for many reasons, not only because of famine and dispossession. Many Americans might be surprised to learn that the first governor proprietor of the state of Maryland, Leonard Calvert, was the second son of a New English—that is, newcomer Irish—aristocrat in County Wexford, George Calvert, the first Lord Baltimore. George Calvert, a Yorkshireman, was himself a major proponent of colonial schemes in both Ireland and North America. The two colonial theaters are thereby linked in one transatlantic history. The only Catholic signatory of the Declaration of Independence, Charles Carroll (1737–1832), was a descendant of the O'Carrolls of Ely, a lordship in the Irish midlands. They were evicted from their property by the early plantation effort in Laois-Offaly (see page 45), begun during the reign of Catholic Queen Mary I in the 1550s. Ironically, the family ended up renewing its fortunes with its plantation in Maryland, named after the same monarch. Nobility and newcomers shaped our nation in surprising ways.

Famously (and infamously), the diaspora caused by the Great Famine in the mid-nineteenth century flooded our shores with Mac's and O's, not to mention Reagans, Kennedys, and even an Obama (via his Kearney ancestors). Many of these Americans have returned to visit "the Old Sod" in search of their ancestors. Queen Elizabeth II's visit to Ireland was immediately followed, the very next week, by President Barack Obama's. Whereas the Queen visited Cashel "of the Kings," a prominent royal and ecclesiastical site, as well as Trinity College Dublin (founded by Queen Elizabeth I) and the English Market in Cork, Obama stopped in the tiny town of Moneygall, County Offaly, and there met his eighth cousin Henry Healy, whom he dubbed "Henry the Eighth." He then addressed a monster rally in front of the old parliament building in Dublin (fig. 7) and spoke of the warm welcome the abolitionist Frederick Douglass had received in Ireland one hundred and sixty-five years earlier. Both rulers, both newcomers, continued the noble tradition of cultural interchange between nations.

FIGURE 7 President Barack Obama and First Lady Michelle Obama attend a rally on May 23, 2011, in College Green, Dublin. Photo by Peter Macdiarmid–Getty Images.

NOBILITY AND NEWCOMERS IN RENAISSANCE IRELAND: A ROYAL "PROGRESS"

THIS CATALOG, like the exhibition, is loosely laid out according to geography and chronology. In the exhibition, the visitor enters from the east end of the hall, which conveniently corresponds with the geographical location of both London and Dublin relative to the rest of Ireland. He or she then circulates through the hall in a clockwise direction, via spaces roughly aligned with the four main provinces in Ireland: Leinster (in the center and southeast of the island), Munster (in the south and southwest), Connacht (in the west and northwest), and Ulster (in the north and northeast). In ancient history, there was a fifth province, Meath (meaning "middle"), dubbed "royal Meath" today: It holds the Hill of Tara, the inaugural site of the high kings of all of Ireland. (Meath is now a county, not a province.) Its placement would correspond symbolically with the center of the hall.

The catalog emphasizes links between Irish and English nobility and places. The progress therefore begins chronologically and geographically with late-medieval to late-Tudor London (chapter 1,

corresponding to case 1 in the exhibit) before moving on to early- to late-Tudor Dublin and the Pale (chapters 2 and 3), and so on.

The progress does not therefore read in teleological fashion and "end" in any one place, but instead returns to Dublin and London, where the reader or visitor can start the circle all over again.

The traffic pattern is a symbolic one. The visitor mimics the traditional progress of a high king of Ireland around the island in a clockwise direction. But rather than starting out in, say, Tara, he or she begins in London and Dublin, the traditional seats of English-Irish administration from the later Middle Ages on, and continues south from there. The visitor therefore *becomes,* in virtual terms, a migrant from London to Ireland, and also "rules" Ireland by "encompassing" and comprehending it, by progressing through its regions and learning about its history. The visitor thereby adopts both a noble's perspective and that of a newcomer.

THE
Firſt part of the Con=

tention betwixt the two famous Houſes of Yorke
and Lancaſter, with the death of the good
Duke Humphrey:

And the baniſhment and death of the Duke of
Suffolke, and the Tragicall end of the proud Cardinall
of *VVincheſter*, vvith the notable Rebellion
of *Iacke Cade*:

And the Duke of Yorkes firſt claime vnto the
Crowne.

LONDON.
Printed by Thomas Creed, for Thomas Millington,
and are to be ſold at his ſhop vnder Saint Peters
Church in Cornwall.
1594.

FIGURE 1.1 William Shakespeare (1564–1616). *King Henry VI. Part 2*
(London: Thomas Creed, 1594), title page. Folger Shelf Mark STC 26099.

1
REBELLION, FANTASY, AND ROYAL ADMINISTRATION: LONDON AND IRELAND,
C. 1450–1603

Enter York, wearing the white rose, *and his army of Irish, with Attendants, Drum and Colors.*

York. From Ireland thus comes York to claim his right
And pluck the crown from feeble Henry's head.
Ring, bells, aloud! Burn, bonfires, clear and bright
To entertain great England's lawful king![12]

A LTHOUGH MODERN OBSERVERS know England and Ireland as separate nations, the interactions between them, especially at the elite level, were intimate and enduring. Contrary to general assumptions, Ireland affected England's high politics just as England affected Ireland's.

English politics in the medieval period, for example, bore a heavy Irish influence. In his *First Part of the Contention of the Two Famous Houses of York and Lancaster with the Death of the Good Duke Humphrey,* also known as the second part of *Henry VI* (1590–1; published 1594; fig. 1.1), Shakespeare emphasizes the Irish backdrop to Jack Cade's rebellion in Kent, England, in 1450. This uprising against the monarchy demonstrated the weakness of Henry VI's kingship and spurred English nobles to call for the royal heir, Richard Duke of York, to return from

Dublin to London and serve as "protector" of the realm (see the quotation above). Rather than plucking the crown, however, York sparked the long-running battle of succession known as the Wars of the Roses.

In this regard, Cade and York resemble many in a venerable line of nobles, major and minor, English and Irish, real and imposters, who used the Irish Sea advantageously: as a platform by which to cross over and manipulate their allegiances and identities in order to legitimize themselves and grow in power. During his rebellion, the commoner Cade took on the name Mortimer, that of a noble family with deep Irish connections who supported the house of York. York, according to Shakespeare's play, was in cahoots with Cade, and both sought material support in Ireland in their efforts at regime change in London. In reality, the extent of York's collusion with Cade, if any, is unknown, but both represented a serious danger to the crown. These men, thus, were simultaneously foreign and domestic threats to England's security and identity, and at the same time fashioned their own identities in an Irish context to suit themselves and their ambitions.

The legitimacy controversy that plagued England's monarchy during the Wars of the Roses did not end with Cade's death, in 1451, or even with that of York nine years later. In spite of the emergence of the house of Tudor following victory at Bosworth Field in 1485, Yorkists

4

572 Polyd. Verg. Ang. hist. lib. XXVI.

instituendum curauit, deditǭ fundos, ad eorum victum. Vocatur Reginæ collegium, eo ipso certè dignum nomine, quod omni tempore doctissimis hominibus ibidem assiduo studio eruditis affluit. Sed ad rem reuertamur.

Rex dimisso concilio, Londinum venit, ac insequenti die dominico, educi per mediam vrbem, ex turri, iussit Edouardum filium ducis Clarentiǫ, ad templum diui Pauli. Hic adolescens, vt edoctus erat, sese omnibus ostendens, interfuit in supplicatione, in cæterisǭ sacris, ac simul collocutus est cum multis principibus, & præsertim cum iis, qui coniurationis participes habebantur, quò illi faciliùs intelligerent Hybernos ex re vana, nouos dementer facere motus. Sed animis malè sanis nihil hæc profuit medicina: nanǭ Ioannes comes Lincolniensis, Ioannis Polæ ducis Suthfolchiæ & Elizabeth Edouardi regis sororis filius, hanc nouandarum rerum facultatem haudquaquã omittendam ratus, statuit Hybernorum conatus, vt ne malè caderent, modis omnibus corroborandos. Sanè vir ingenij acrimoniǫ pleni, & consilij non modici, veneno ciuilium inimicitiarũ iampridem infectus, non poterat in animum suum inducere, vt patienter videret Henricum aduersæ factionis hominem regnare, qui propterea inito cum Thoma Brogtono, ac plerisǭ aliis amicis consilio, decreuit ad Margaritam materteram traiicere, & eius opibus nixus, ad nouæ seditionis autores adhærescere. Itaǭ statim post dimissum à rege principum conuentum, comes clàm in Flãdriam ad Margaritam venit, quò aliquot antè diebus, Franciscus Louellus se receperat. Hic pro suo quisǭ sensu ac desiderio, in rerum gerendarum rationem locutus est, quarum post longam disputatione, summa fuit, vt comes cum Frãcisco properè Hyberniam peteret, Lambertum fictitium nepotem regio honore honestandum curaret, Hybernorum auxilia cum nouo rege, in Angliam adduceret, amicis vndiǭ ad arma vocatis, bellum Henrico faceret, & si res feliciter caderet, tum Lamberto in ordinem redacto, Edouardum comite Varuicensem verum nepotẽ carcere primùm liberaret, ac postea ex autoritate principum amicorum, regem constitueret. Rex Henricus interim, qui sperabat suos principes post visum Edouardũ filiũ ducis Clarentiæ quieturos, nec esse quempiam tam improbũ putabat, qui de eo quicǭ fingeret, nec tam furiosum, qui crederet, solùm studebat Hybernorũ temeritatẽ cõpescere, cùm repentè de fuga comitis Lincolniensis cognouit, qui ob eam rem valdè animi perturbatione cõmotus, inimicorũ iniurias quas nullo cõsilio vitare se posse animaduertebat, iam tum apertè persequendas, vindicandásǭ armis statuit: itaǭ certos belli duces quaquauersum missos exercitũ parare, atǭ in vnum locũ cogere iussit, vt omni multitudine in eam partẽ impressionẽ facerent, quà aduersarios venire constiterit: ipse interim timens ne non plures in Flãdriam ad comitẽ transfugerent, omnem oram quæ ad orientem solem spectat, obire passim præsidiis, custodiis, vigiliisǭ munire cœpit, & iam ad cœnobiũ diui Edmundi peruenerat, cùm intellexit Thomã marchionem sui purgãdi causa ad se approperare, quem misso obuiàm Ioanne comite Oxoniensi, de itinere in turrim Londinensem duci iussit, vt si esset amicus, sicuti reuera erat, illud tantillũ indignitatis eius salutis causa subire, haud ægrè ferret: sin inimicus, ne noceret: quo facto, Nordouicũ petit, & ibi Christi die natali acto, Vualsingamiam progreditur, ingressusǭ diuæ Virginis templum, quod in eo pago ob summam miraculorum religionem, sanctissimũ est, orat, precatur, atǭ
vota

Henricus septimus. 573

vota facit, vt ope diuina, & virginis Mariǫ ductu, sibi liceat inimicorũ insidias cauere, & se & patriam ab instanti periculo defendere, eiusǭ vitiosas partes sanare. Ita precatus Cantabrigiam & inde Londinum celeriter reuertitur.

Interea Ioannes comes Lincolniensis & Frãciscus Louellus, accepto à Margarita exercitu duorum circiter milliũ Germanorũ, quibus præerat Martinus Suardus homo Germanus, summo genere natus, ac rei bellicæ scientia præstans, in Hyberniam traiiciunt, atǭ Dublini Lambertum puerum perinde quasi regia stirpe ortum, more maiorũ, regem creandum curant. Post hæc, Hybernorum egentium ac ferè inermium coacta ingenti multitudine, quorum dux erat Thomas Gerardinus, cum nouo rege, in Angliam nauigant, ac dedita opera, haud à Lancastro procul in terram descendunt, freti opibus Thomæ Brogtoni, qui princeps erat coniurationis socius. Rex aũt Henricus qui suæ caulæ non indormiebat, quod acciderat suspicatus, paulò ante aduentum hostium, dimiserat per oram ad occidentẽ spectantẽ, aliquot equitũ turmas, cùm ad obseruãdum aduersariorum accessum, tum ad aliquos de Hybernia profectos excipiendos, ex quibus hostium consilia cognosceret, & ipse copiis coactis, quibus Gasparẽ Bedfordiæ ducẽ, & Ioannẽ Oxoniensem comitem præfecerat, Couentriam petebat, quò vix peruenerat, cùm equites officio functi renuntiarunt comitem cum suo collectitio exercitu, ac nouo rege, in oram Lãcastrensem esse appulsum: quod vbi intellexit, de obuiàm itione, cum suo domestico senatu agit, cùm res nõ inanis videretur postulare consiliũ pariter ac celeritatem. Cunctis vna mente probatur, vt ipse aduersarios venientes excipiat, quoquo gentiũ ierint, seǭ receperint, ne illis spatium detur maioris faciẽdi exercitus. Ita capro consilio, rex Nothyngamiã petit, ad proximãmǭ syluã, quæ Bonrys vocitatur, castra ponit, quò non multò post cum magno armatorum numero conuenit Georgius Talbotus comes Salopiensis, Georgius regulus Strangius, ac Ioannes Chenius, egregij belli gloria duces, cũ pluribus aliis rei militaris peritissimis: nam Henricus ex vicinis comitatibus nobilissimũ & fortissimũ queǭ partim ad se euocarat, partim iusserat, vt qui arma ferre possent, quamparatissimi forent, subsidio venire, si opus esset. Itaque vno propè tempore habito militũ delectu, magnæ copiæ coactæ sunt, quarũ centuriones & duces erant, Rodulphus Longfordius, Ioannes Montigomerius, Henricus Vernonus ex Pek, Rodulphus Shurleius, Gotthofredus Folgehan, Thomas Grysleius, Edouardus Suttonus, Humfredus Stanleius, alter Humfredus Stanleius, Gulielmus Hugtonus, Gulielmus Meryngus, Edouardus Stanopus, Geruasius Clystonus, Brianus Stapultonus, Henricus Vuyllugby, Gulielmus Perpoynt, Ioannes Babyngtonus, Gulielmus Bedyllus, Robertus Brundellus, Ioannes Markham, Gulielmus Merbury, Edouardus Aborogh, Gulielmus Tyruuitus, Ioannes Huseius, Robertus Shefildus, Gulielmus Neuportus, Rogerius Ormestonus, Thomas Tempesta, Gulielmus Knyuettus, Henricus Vuyllugby, Edouardus Hastyngius regulus, Ioannes Dygby, Simon Dygby Haryngtonus, Ricardus Sacheuerellus, Ioannes Vyllers, Edouardus Fyldyngus, Thomas Pulteneius, Nicolaus Vaux, Thomas Grynus, Nicolaus Gryhnus, Edmũdus Lucy, Edouardus Belknapus, Robertus Throgmartonus, Georgius Graius è Ruthyn, Guido Volstonus, Thomas Fynderius, Dauid Philippus, Thomas Cheneius, Robertus Cottonus, Ioãnes sancti

FIGURE 1.2 Polydore Vergil (1470?–1555). *Anglica Historia* (Basel: Thomas Guarin, 1570), 572–73. Folger Shelf Mark Folio PA8585.V4 A3 1570 Cage.

FIGURE 1.3 John Payne. *Henry VII*
(London: W. Stansby, 1622).
Folger Shelf Mark ART Box P346 no. 1 (size S).

FIGURE 1.4 French School. Portrait of Perkin Warbeck (c. 1474–99), Flemish imposter and pretender to the English throne. (16th century), sanguine on paper. Courtesy of Bibliothèque Municipale/The Bridgeman Art Library.

still coveted the crown and would launch two more challenges in pursuit of it from strongholds in Ireland. Polydore Vergil, an Italian humanist in the employ of Henry VII, relates the failed 1486 coup d'état of Lambert Simnel and his promoters in his propagandistic history, *Anglicae Historia* (1534; fig. 1.2). Simnel, thought to have been the son of an Oxford artisan, was the pawn of nobles who opposed the new Tudor regime. The boy was taken out of Oxford and into Ireland, where he was promoted by (and to) Yorkist supporters as the throne's rightful heir. After being proclaimed King of England before a Dublin crowd, he, his supporters, and more than five thousand German and Irish troops landed in England with the goal of regime change in London. The coup d'état failed and Simnel was mercifully employed by Henry VII (fig. 1.3) as a kitchen boy. Vergil, not surprisingly, dismisses Simnel as a "pretender" and his supporters as "treasonous."

Simnel was followed by Perkin Warbeck (fig. 1.4), another commoner and doomed pretender, who claimed the English throne as

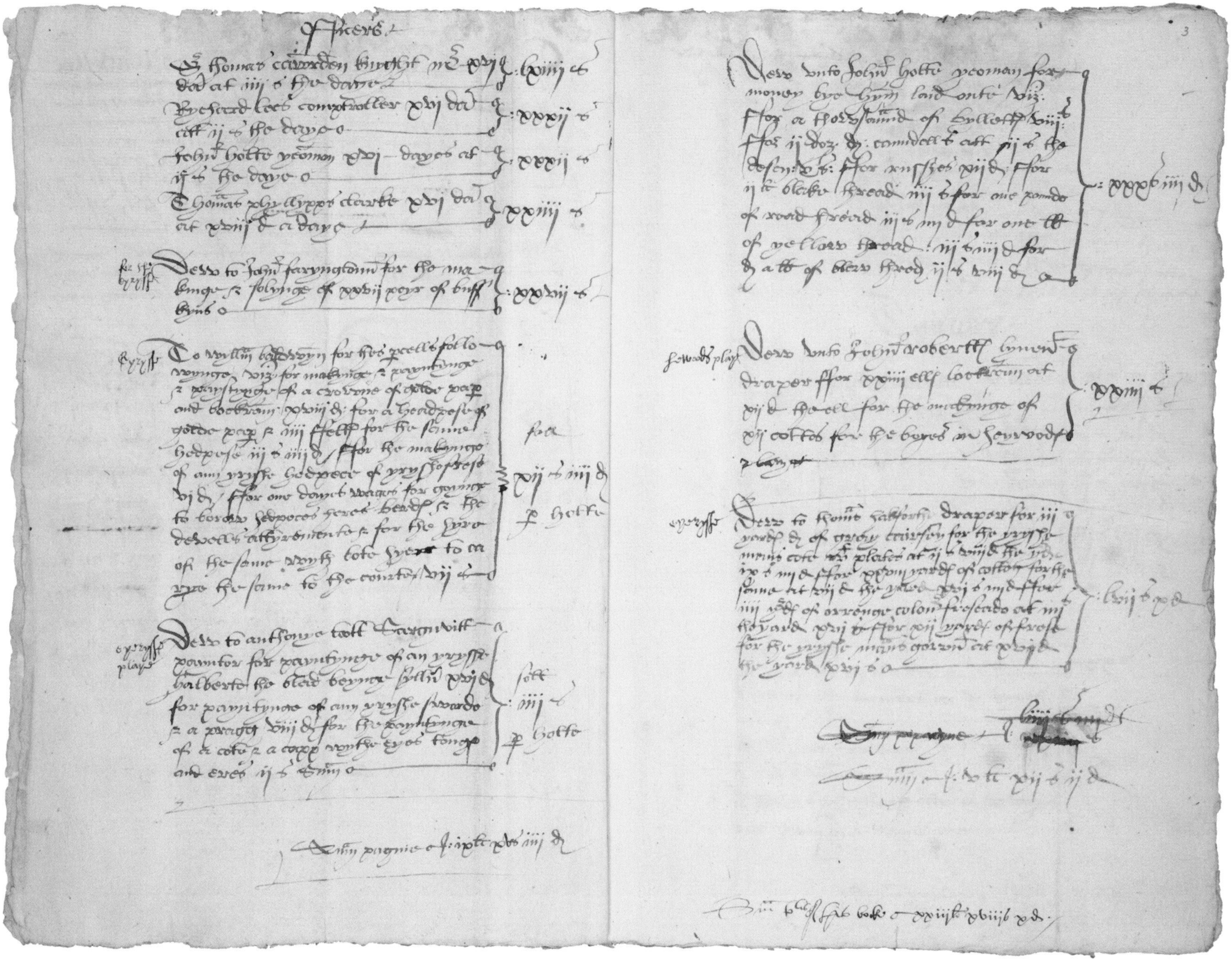

FIGURE 1.5 Great Britain. Office of the Revels. Revells ffrom shrovetide, 1554/1555, sig. 2v–3r. Folger Shelf Mark L.b.302.

Richard Plantagenet, Duke of York. He launched his campaign against Henry VII from the town of Cork in 1492, and was feted by powers in Ireland, Scotland, Cornwall, parts of England, and the Continent. Bested on the field, then discovered plotting from his cell in the Tower of London, Warbeck ended his life in a noose in 1499. (The playwright John Ford would eventually base a play, *Perkin Warbeck* [1634], on his exploits; see page 104.) Whatever Vergil's opinion of Simnel's uprising and the later one involving Warbeck, both actions demonstrated Londoners' need to take Ireland into account in any consideration of high politics and succession.

England's view of Ireland was fantastic and pragmatic and not a little fearful, and Ireland and the Irish inhabited the imaginative, as well as the political, world of Londoners. We tend to think of the stage Irishman—a stock character played for laughs—as a seventeenth-century development. An Office of the Revels account book (fig. 1.5), however, reveals a much earlier example of Irish characters in English drama. It describes the props and costumes required for an "eyeryshe playe" performed before Edward VI in 1553, including a "payntynge of an yryshe halberte the blad beynge sylluer."[13] This is thought to be for William Baldwin's lost "Play of the State of Ireland."

The Irish themselves were frequently fantasized about by Londoners as belonging to a wild and savage world. The English translation (1591) by Sir John Harington of that early-modern "best seller," Ludovico Ariosto's Italian romance-epic *Orlando Furioso* (figs. 1.6, 1.7), describes Irish lords in fantastic circumstances—situations visually represented by an image of a protagonist flying over an island of monsters and natural wonders en route to Ireland, another exotic place at the edge of the known world. A staged version of the Orlando story by Robert Greene, *The Historie of Orlando Furioso, One of the Twelve Peeres of France* (1594; reprinted 1599), places Orlando in a forest surrounded by satyrs, enchanted by the sorceress Melissa, and serenaded on the fiddle by Shan, perhaps a version of Shane (like Sean, an Irish version of

74

Then come the Irish men of valiant harts,
Actiue in limbs, in personages tall,
Naked they vse to go in manie parts,
But with a mantell yet they couer all:
Short swords they vse to carrie and long darts,
To fight both neare and farre aloofe withall,
And of these bands the Lords and leaders are,
The noble Earls of Ormond and Kildare.

FIGURE 1.6 Ludovico Ariosto. *Orlando Furioso* (London: Richard Field, 1591), 78, stanza 74. Folger Shelf Mark STC 746 copy 1.

the English name John). Crazy Orlando, thinking the fiddle a sword and himself in danger, breaks it on Shan's head: not the first or last misunderstanding of Irish intentions by travelers in that country.

Sir John Harington would himself fight against Ireland in England's armies at the end of the 1590s. While there, he read portions of his Ariosto translation to the arch-rebel Hugh O'Neill, Earl of Tyrone, and his sons, and debated theology with their priest. A good laugh must have been shared concerning Ariosto's notion of Ireland as part of a bizarre and wondrous world.

This idea of a "fantastical Ireland" should not lead us to think that the English in fact knew little about the island and its inhabitants. The map of Ireland in Camden's historical magnum opus, *Britannia* (1600; see fig. 1.8), reveals the London government's emerging cartographic certainty regarding the island as a place it needed to better understand in order to govern, reconquer, and recolonize. The twinned images of Ireland in English consciousness nonetheless persisted: seat of provincial power (much like the north of England) and home to an exotic "other" against which a sense of Englishness could be developed.

7

THE TENTH BOOKE

10

92

But now *Rogero* doth this sleight deuise,
Sith that by force he cannot make him yeeld,
He means to dasell both the monsters eyes,
By hidden force of his enchaunted sheeld,
And being thus resolu'd to land he flies,
And from all harme the Ladie faire to sheeld,
He puts the precious ring vpon her hand,
Whose vertue was enchauntments to withstand.

93

That ring that worthie *Bradamant* him sent,
When she from false *Brunello* had it tane,
With which *Melissa* into India went,
And wrought his freedome, and *Alcynas* bane,
That ring he lends the damsell with intent,
To saue her eyes by vertue of the same:
Then takes he foorth the sheeld whose light so da-
The lookers-on they fall downe all amazed. (zed,

94

The monster now approching to the shore,
Amazd at this, resistance none did make,
Rogero hews vpon him more and more,
But his hard scales no harme therby did take.
Oh sir (said she) vnloosen me before,
Out of this maze the monster do awake,
And let your sword slay me this present houre,
So as this monster may not me deuoure.

95

These woful words mou'd so *Rogeros* mind,
That straight he did vnloose the Ladie faire,
And caus'd her by and by to get behind,
Vpon his horse, then mounting in the aire,
He leaues his Spanish iourney first assignd,
And vnto litle Britein doth repaire,
But by the way be sure he did not misse,
To giue her many a sweet and friendly kisse.

96

And hauing found a solitarie place,
A pleasant groue well watered with a spring,
Which neuer herd nor herdman did deface,
Where *Philomela* vsed still to sing,
Here he alights, minding to stay a space,
And hither he the Ladie faire did bring,
But sure it seemd he made his full account,
Er long vpon a better beast to mount.

97

His armour made him yet a while to byde,
Which forced stay, a more desire did breed,
But now in him it was most truly tryde,
Oftimes the greater hast, the worse the speed,
He knits with hast two knots, while one vntyde.
But soft tis best no furder to proceede,
Now I cut of abruptly here my rime,
And keepe my tale vnto another time.

Sentence.

Moral. In *Byreno* that abandoned his kinde *Olympia* in a desolate Iland, and fell in loue with another, we may note an example of ingratitude, the monstrous fault of all faults, most odious before God and man: and herein learne to abhorre and
detest this vice in him and in all others, that hauing receaued preferment and aduancement, either by men or women, when
they haue done, shake them off like horses that be lame, or garments that be old, preferring one to the rest the other to the dung-
hill: or as our *Stukley* said, make as much of his wife as he could, if any could make more of her they might take her, after
he had gotten many thousand pounds by making much of her. In the spitefull words that one of *Alcynas* women spake of *Rogero*, we may obserue the maner of wanton woodlings, that if they see a young man liue temperatly, or go plainly, or speake de-
uoutly, straight they say he is a base fellow and one that knowes not what belongs to a Gentleman, which foolish maner of
phrase by *Rogeros* example we must learne to contemne, and know that such men are indeede base as thinke temperance and
sobrietie and deuotion base qualities. Finally in *Rogeros* trauell about the world, we may see how commendable it is for a yong
Gentleman to trauell abrode into forraine nations: but yet we may note withall an inconuenience, that comes many times with
it, to see some *Angelicas* naked that will tempt men of very stanch gouernment and stayd yeers, to that which they shall after
repent, as *Rogero* did this his wantonnesse, as appears more plainly in the next booke, where you shall find he lost both his horse
and the ring by the vngratefulnesse of *Angelica*.

Historie. For the matter historicall of this tenth booke there is litle to be sayd, and nothing to be affirmed: for the succors sent to France
from England, Scotland, Ireland, and manie places there abouts, though I can not affirme precisely of the time, yet sure it is that
manie haue bene sent hence against the Turke to France and elsewhere. And whereas he speakes of S. Patricke the Irish saint,
I would haue them that would know the storie of him to looke in *Surius de vitis sanctorū*, and there they may see it at large:
for mine owne part at my being in Ireland where I taried a few moneths, I was inquisitiue of their opinion of this Saint, and I
could learne nothing, other then a reuerent conceipt that they had of him as becomes all Christians to haue of deuout men, and
chiefly of those by whom they are first instructed in the Christian faith: but for his purgatorie I found neither any that affirmed it or beleeued it.

Allegorie. *Logestillas* castell, the ornaments therof, the herbs of the garden, all these figure the true magnificense, glorie, con sort, and
ciuilitie of vertue. The foure Ladies sent to rescue *Rogero*, are the foure Cardinall vertues, which being well vnited togeth er,
are able to ouerthrow whole nauies of vicious pleasures; and so what so euer else is spoken of *Logestilla* in Allegorie is taken
for vertue.

Allusion. In *Angelica* tyde to the rocks and deliuered by *Rogero*, he alludes manifestly to the tale in *Ouid* of *Andromade* and
Perseus who with his shield turned the beholders into stones.

8

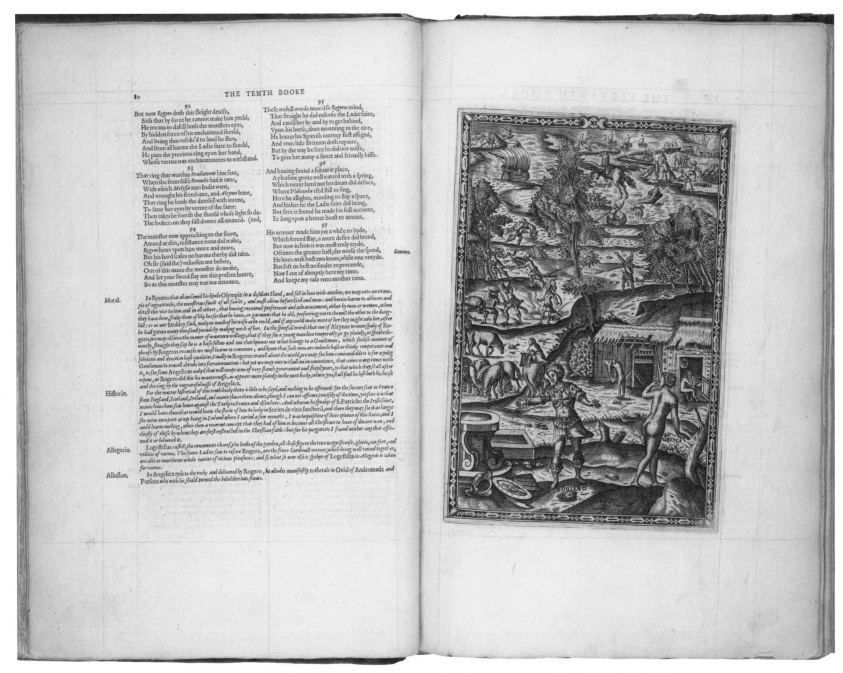

FIGURE 1.7 Ludovico Ariosto. *Orlando Furioso* (London: Richard Field, 1591), 80–81. Folger Shelf Mark STC 746 copy 1.

HIBERNIA. 755

Ireland.

N Vergiuio mari, quod non à ver-
gendo, vt Cheneius Scotus existi-
mat, deducitur, sed à *Mor Weridh*,
hoc enim nomine Britannis dici-
tur, vel à *Farigi* quo pro mari illo
vtuntur Hibernici, Britanniæ no-
stræ latus occiduum claudit cele-
berrima insula vulgò HIBERNIA
dicta, Orpheo, Aristoteli, & Clau-
diano IERNA, Iuuenali & Melæ
IVVERNA, Diodoro Siculo IRIS,
Eustathio Ουεργία, & Βερνία, incolis *Erin*, Britannis *Yuerdon*, & no-
bis Anglis *Ireland*. Vnde hæc profluxerunt nomina, variæ vt in
re obscura subinde enatæ sunt opiniones. Hiberniam alij ab hiberno tempore, alij ab Hibero homine Hispano, ab Ibero flu-
mine alij, Eulogij author ab Irnalpho Duce, Postellus dum Me-
lam Lutetiæ nuper prælegeret, vt altum sapere videretur, ab He-
bræis repetit, vt sit *Irin*, quasi *Iurin*, id est, *Hebræorum terra*, Hebræi
(inquit si dijs placet) cùm essent Magi peritissimi, scirentque Impe-
rium Uniuersi futurum in angulo fortissimo, qui est ad Caurum, illas
partes, & Hiberniam quàm primùm occuparunt, Syrique & Tyrij illas
regiones vt basim futuri imperij ponerent, incolere sategerunt. Ignosce
quæso si his suffragari non ausim, ne receptissimæ quidem isti de
hiberno tempore opinioni, quamuis legerim in hac Insula ex
omni vento aërem brumescere. *Hibernia, Iuuerna*, & Ουεργία pro-
culdubio ab Orphei & Aristotelis *Ierna* dimanârunt, *Ierna* autem
illa, *Iris, Iuerdhon*, & *Ireland*, ab incolarum *Erin*. Ab *Erin* ergo gen-
tis vocabulo originatio petenda. Hîc ego cum magnis illis Philo-
sophis ἐπέχω, nec quid opinione augurari possim, habeo : nisi
forsan sit ab *Hiere* Hibernica dictione quæ illis occasum, siue pla-
gam Occidentalem sonat, vnde *Erin* quasi Occidentalis regio
deducta videatur. Hoc ego coniectura blandiente iampridem
putaui, tum quòd totius Europæ regio sit ad Occasum remotis-
sima, (vtpote quæ XII. tantùm partibus ab vltimo Occidente
absit : tum quòd Occidentalissimum huius insulæ flumen Pto-
lemæo *Iernus*, & Occidentalissimum Hispaniæ Promontorium,
vnde nostri Hibernici deuenerunt) IERNE Straboni, proximus-
que

Ccc que

Marginal note (right):
Oceanus Vergiuius.

Map cartouche:
HIBERNIA ANTIQVA
Ierna *Orpheo & Arist.*
Iris *Diodoro Siculo.*
Iuuerna *Iuuenali.*
Yuerdon *Britannis.*
Ireland *Anglis.*
Erin *Incolis.*

FIGURE 1.8 William Camden. *Britannia* (London: George Bishop, 1600), map + page 755. Folger Shelf Mark STC 4507 copy 3.

FIGURE 2.1 John Speed (1552?–1629). *Theatre of the Empire of Great Britaine*
(London: [T. Snodham], 1616), plate between pages 137 and 138: Map of Ireland. Folger Shelf Mark STC 23044.

2
OLD ENGLISH LORDS AND NEW ENGLISH ADMINISTRATION: TUDOR DUBLIN, C. 1485–1603

CROSSING THE IRISH SEA and alighting in Dublin, the traveler immediately comprehends how English and Irish noble connections played out there as they did in London—at times harmonious, at times violently contentious. Dublin was always an international city. Founded by marauding and trading Vikings in the ninth century, it became the de facto capital of the island by the time of its conquest by England in the late twelfth century (fig. 2.1). These conquerors, ambitious English- and French-speaking Anglo-Normans from England and Wales looking to improve their wealth and status by capturing new territories, were led by Richard de Clare, a.k.a. Strongbow.

Shortly after defeating his Irish opponents, Strongbow greatly advanced his potential power by marrying the daughter of Diarmait Mac Murchada, King of Leinster and claimant to the Irish High Kingship. Henry II of England, fearing that Strongbow would turn rival king in the neighboring island, took matters into his own hands and journeyed to Ireland to win the political loyalty of Strongbow, his supporters, and the greater Irish nobility. A "conquest" it was, albeit in fits and starts, and it set the precedent for intimate connections—by blood, marriage, and alliance—between nominally "English" and nominally "Irish" grandees.

Although descendants of the twelfth-century Anglo-Norman colonists thought of themselves as English, the sixteenth century saw a new level of complexity added to that identity, and to Dublin politics more generally. In 1541, Ireland was made a kingdom under the English crown (a constitutional change enacted in both the English and the Irish parliaments). All of the island's inhabitants were now subjects.

Gaelic lords were invited to the imperial centers, Dublin and London, to "surrender" their traditional titles and lands and have them "regranted" back according to English law. Thus, for example, the head of the O'Neills became the Earl of Tyrone and the head of the O'Briens became the Earl of Thomond. Old English nobles also took advantage of "surrender and regrant" opportunities to strengthen their ties with the crown. The chief of the Galway Burkes negotiated for a new title— the Earl of Clanricard—and the Earl of Desmond made a pilgrimage to court simply to reconfirm his title. More dramatic still was the injection of a whole new class of English place-seekers and aspiring power brokers into Irish politics. The Kingdom of Ireland was flooded by a wave of "New" English subjects, including administrators, officers, churchmen, and soldiers. They challenged the authority of those "Old English" power brokers, descended from the original Anglo-Norman conquerors, who believed local supremacy to be their birthright.

This tension was exacerbated by religious divergence. Despite their initial sympathy for Henry VIII's ecclesiastical innovations during the Protestant Reformation, the great majority of the "Old English" descendants would prove staunch Catholics. The newcomers, on the other hand, overwhelmingly favored the reformed religion of the Tudor state. The English government based in Dublin therefore had a difficult task ahead of it: how to better govern and convert, if it could, a conservative populace mostly loyal to the crown but firmly dissenting in their spiritual practices, a local population wary of carpetbaggers or new men who brought radical changes in their monarch's name.

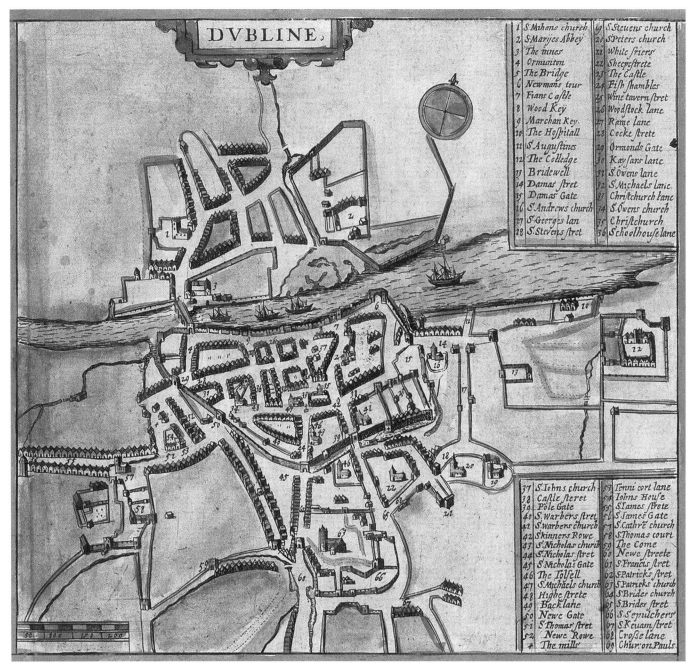

FIGURE 2.2 *Civitates Orbis Terrarum* ([Cologne: Anton Hierat & Abraham Hogenberg, 1618?]). Folger Shelf Mark ART 229985.

FIGURE 2.3A Raphael Holinshed (d. 1580?). *Chronicles of England, Scotlande, and Irelande* (London: [Henry Bynneman, 1577]), detail from page 84. Folger Shelf Mark STC 13567.8 vol. 1.

FIGURE 2.3B Raphael Holinshed (d. 1580?). *Chronicles of England, Scotlande, and Irelande,* detail from page 94. Folger Shelf Mark STC 13567.8 vol. 1.

Nowhere was this contest between elite groups — separated, ironically, by a common "English" identity—more intense than in the viceregal seat of Dublin (fig. 2.2). As the rebellions of Simnel and Warbeck demonstrated (see pages 5, 7), controlling Dublin and its elites was crucial to maintaining peace in the realms. Raphael Holinshed's *Chronicles of England, Scotlande, and Irelande* (1577) graphically illustrates the viceregal majesty of the Lord Deputy and his punitive power over the resident nobility. An initial woodcut shows Lord Deputy Sir William Skeffington, accompanied by the Earl of Kildare, welcomed at the walls of Dublin by the city's residents (fig. 2.3A). Mistrust and tension between the King and the Earl would in time lead Kildare to revolt, and the second picture shows the Earl's forces besieging the capital (fig. 2.3B). Holinshed was keen to demonstrate that crime against the crown did not pay, and the final image sees the rebellious earl on the executioner's block (fig. 2.3C).

FIGURE 2.3C Raphael Holinshed (d. 1580?). *Chronicles of England, Scotlande, and Irelande,* detail from page 98. Folger Shelf Mark STC 13567.8 vol. 1.

FIGURE 2.4 John Derricke. *Image of Irelande* (London: [J. Kingston], 1581), plate 6: Sidney leading troops from Dublin Castle. Courtesy of the University of Edinburgh.

The need for a viceregal taming of the local nobility—which we must remember was traditionally a warrior class—is sharply demonstrated. The same principle was well understood by Sir Henry Sidney, thrice Lord Deputy of Ireland under Elizabeth, father of the noted poets Philip and Mary, and a prolific writer himself. Sidney was a master at propaganda, building bridges and monuments in Dublin and farther afield that bore his and the monarchy's arms and patronizing literary works that celebrated his iron, and orthodox, rule. John Derricke's lavishly illustrated Protestant polemic, *The Image of Irelande* (1581),[14] portrays Sidney leading troops from Dublin Castle—the administrative seat of crown power—on their way to engage Irish rebels on the fringes of the Pale: that is, the hinterland around Dublin ruled effectively by the crown.

In this woodcut (fig. 2.4), Dublin looks well built and, by impli-

14

cation, well run. The tall spire of Christ Church Cathedral, a vital center of Protestant worship and administration, is the highest point on the skyline. The deputy's muscular and Anglicizing governorship is celebrated in Derricke's accompanying caption and throughout the lengthy main poem. At the end of the second part, for example, his chivalric fame is trumpeted in doggerel verse that paradoxically equates war with peace:

> Sir Henry is renowmde
>> with fame unto the Skie:
> And is receiv'de to Dublin toune,
>> prais'de for his cheualrie.
> Thus peace ensewes by warre,
>> the ende of warre is peace.
> God graunt the warres of Irishe soile,
>> by *Sidneys* meanes maie cease.[15]

Sidney was not afraid to burn the village in order to save it, and Derricke does not shy away from celebrating his martial accomplishments. Derricke is also guilty of wishful thinking. The Lord Deputy's scorched-earth tactics against the Gaels of the midlands were effective, but his heavy-handed taxation of the Old English of Dublin and the Pale to pay for these campaigns caused serious discontent. In other areas of the country, as in the Earl of Ormond's territory to the southwest, Sidney's policies led to outright rebellion by his Old English lords (in this instance, the brothers of the Earl of Ormond).

Although the Lord Deputy of Ireland had extraordinary authority, unmatched by English viceregal authorities in other parts of the realms—say, the north of England and the Welsh Marches—he nonetheless took orders from London. In a letter to Henry Sidney (fig. 2.5), Elizabeth I commands him to remove and discharge Thomas Stukeley (the famous adventurer killed at the Battle of Alcazar in 1578) as seneschal, or governor, of Wexford, and replace him with Nicholas

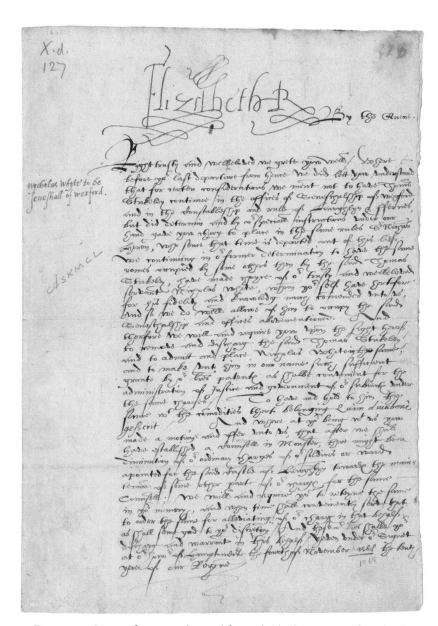

FIGURE 2.5 Letter of command signed from Elizabeth I, Queen of England, to Sir Henry Sidney, Lord Deputy of Ireland: November 4, 1568. Folger Shelf Mark X.d.127.

15

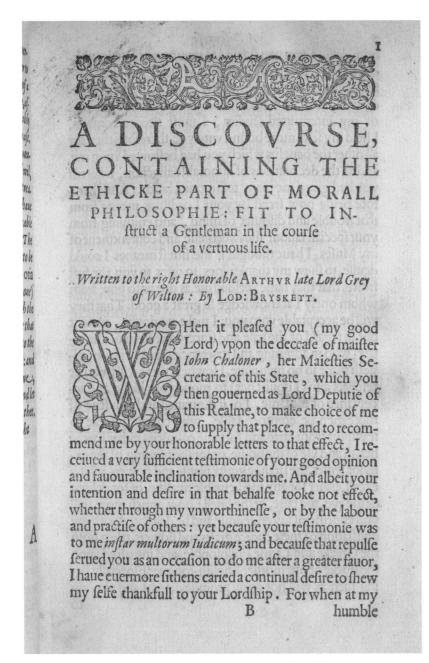

I

A DISCOVRSE, CONTAINING THE ETHICKE PART OF MORALL PHILOSOPHIE: FIT TO IN-
struct a Gentleman in the course of a vertuous life.

Written to the right Honorable ARTHVR *late Lord Grey of Wilton :* By LOD: BRYSKETT.

Hen it pleased you (my good Lord) vpon the deccase of maister *Iohn Chaloner* , her Maiesties Se-cretarie of this State , which you then gouerned as Lord Deputie of this Realme, to make choice of me to supply that place, and to recom-mend me by your honorable letters to that effect , I re-ceiued a very sufficient testimonie of your good opinion and fauourable inclination towards me. And albeit your intention and desire in that behalfe tooke not effect, whether through my vnworthinesse , or by the labour and practise of others : yet because your testimonie was to me *instar multorum Iudicum* ; and because that repulse serued you as an occasion to do me after a greater fauor, I haue euermore sithens caried a continual desire to shew my selfe thankfull to your Lordship . For when at my humble

A   B

FIGURE 2.6 Lodowick Bryskett, *A Discourse of civill life* (London: William Aspley, 1606), sig. B1r. Folger Shelf Mark STC 3959.

16

White. Stukeley had been appointed by Sidney, but the queen over-rode his decision.

Dublin was also a seat of great learning and literary experimenta-tion in the later Tudor period. Lodowick Bryskett's *Discourse of Civill Life* (1582?; published 1606; fig. 2.6), an embellished translation of Giambattista Giraldi Cinthio's humanistic dialogue *Tre Dialoghi della Vita Civile* (from *De gli Hecatommithi,* 1565), is set by Bryskett in a southern suburb of Dublin. Bryskett, a New English administrator of English-Italian origin, describes a gathering of (mostly) New English soldiers and administrators, including the poet Edmund Spenser. Here we learn that Spenser is already hard at work on *The Faerie Queene* and that his patron, Arthur, Lord Grey, Sir Henry Sidney's successor as Lord Deputy of Ireland, ran a godly and just administration that set the stage for further reform:

> We have (said *sir Robert Dillon*) great cause indeed to thanke God of the present state of our country . . . My Lord Grey hath plowed and harrowed the rough ground to hand: but you know that he that soweth the seede, whereby we hope for harvest according to the goodnesse of that which is cast into the earth, and the seasonablenesse of the times, deserveth no lesse praise than he that manureth the land.[16]

The rough work of one lord deputy harrows the field for the next in his effort to plant English government and "civill life" in Ireland. Intriguingly, Bryskett's speaker in this instance, Sir Robert Dillon, was a Protestant from a distinguished Old English family of the Pale who served loyally in the administration as Privy Councilor and Chief Jus-tice of the Court of Common Pleas in Ireland. Not all Old English opposed the growing New English hegemony over Dublin, although few profited as much from it as did Dillon.

The English literary Renaissance, then, has a strong Dublin con-nection. Sir Philip Sidney (pictured with his father; figs. 2.7, 2.8),

S.ᴿ PHILIP SIDNEY.

FIGURE 2.7 William Wynne Ryland (1732–83). *Sir Philip Sidney* ([18th century]). Folger Shelf Mark ART File S569 no. 6 (size XS).

FIGURE 2.8 Arnold van Brounkhorst (fl. 1565–1583) [after]. Portrait of Sir Henry Sidney (1529–86), Lord Deputy of Ireland (16th century), oil on panel. Courtesy of the National Gallery of Ireland.

17

author of the great Elizabethan sonnet sequence *Astrophil and Stella* and the lengthy pastoral prose romance the *Arcadia,* also spent time in Ireland, in the summer of 1576. A famous dinner guest on the Continent, it is difficult to imagine him not discussing current fashions in Dublin with companions such as his father and Walter Devereux, first Earl of Essex, who also served there. Philip was later promoted by his father as a candidate for Lord Deputy of Ireland, a post Philip apparently coveted but never took up.

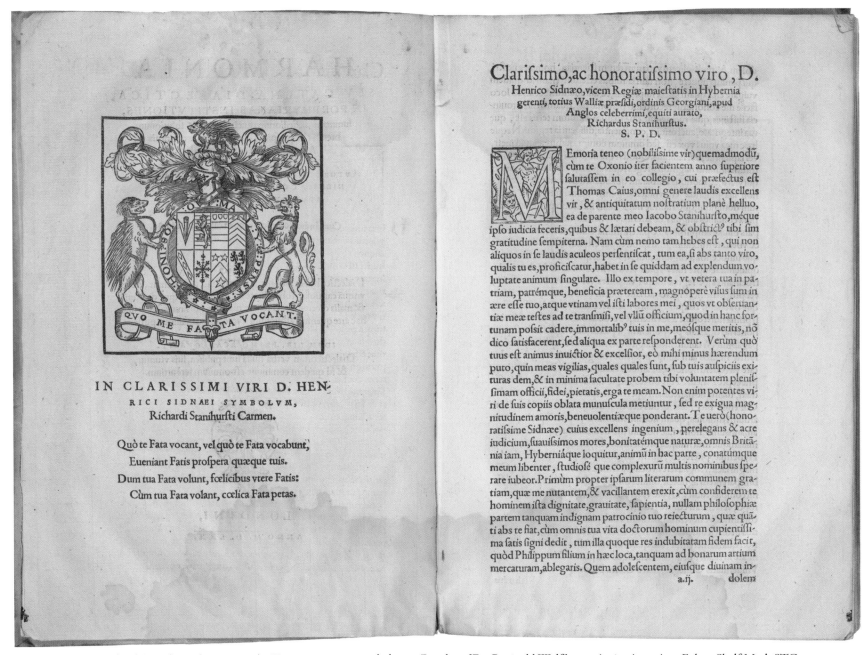

IN CLARISSIMI VIRI D. HEN-
RICI SIDNAEI SYMBOLVM,
Richardi Stanihursti Carmen.

Quò te Fata vocant, vel quò te Fata vocabunt,
Eueniant Fatis prospera quæque tuis.
Dum tua Fata volunt, fœlicibus vtere Fatis:
Cùm tua Fata volant, cœlica Fata petas.

Clarissimo, ac honoratissimo viro, D.
Henrico Sidnæo, vicem Regiæ maiestatis in Hybernia
gerenti, totius Walliæ præsidi, ordinis Georgiani, apud
Anglos celeberrimi, equiti aurato,
Richardus Stanihurstus.
S. P. D.

Emoria teneo (nobilissime vir) quemadmodũ,
cùm te Oxonio iter facientem anno superiore
salutassem in eo collegio, cui præfectus est
Thomas Caius, omni genere laudis excellens
vir, & antiquitatum nostratium planè helluo,
ea de parente meo Iacobo Stanihursto, méque
ipso iudicia feceris, quibus & lætari debeam, & obstrict° tibi sim
gratitudine sempiterna. Nam cùm nemo tam hebes est, qui non
aliquos in se laudis aculeos persentiscat, tum ea, si abs tanto viro,
qualis tu es, proficiscatur, habet in se quiddam ad explendum vo-
luptate animum singulare. Illo ex tempore, vt vetera tua in patriam, patrémque, beneficia præteream, magnóperè visus sum in
ære esse tuo, atque vtinam vel isti labores mei, quos vt obseruan-
tiæ meæ testes ad te transmisi, vel vllũ officium, quod in hanc for-
tunam possit cadere, immortalib° tuis in me, meósque meritis, nõ
dico satisfacerent, sed aliqua ex parte responderent. Verùm quò
tuus est animus inuictior & excelsior, eò mihi minus hærendum
puto, quin meas vigilias, quales quales sunt, sub tuis auspiciis exi-
turas dem, & in minima facultate probem tibi voluntatem plenis-
simam officii, fidei, pietatis, erga te meam. Non enim potentes viri de suis copiis oblata munuscula metiuntur, sed re exigua mag-
nitudinem amoris, beneuolentiæque ponderant. Te uerò (honora-
tissime Sidnæe) cuius excellens ingenium, perelegans & acre
iudicium, suauissimos mores, bonitatémque naturæ, omnis Brita-
nia iam, Hyberniáque loquitur, animũ in hac parte, conatúmque
meum libenter, studiosè que complexurũ multis nominibus spe-
rare iubeor. Primùm propter ipsarum literarum communem gra-
tiam, quæ me nutantem, & vacillantem erexit, cùm considerem te
hominem ista dignitate, grauitate, sapientia, nullam philosophiæ
partem tanquam indignam patrocinio tuo reiecturum, quæ quã-
ti abs te fiat, cùm omnis tua vita doctorum hominum cupientissi-
ma satis signi dedit, tum illa quoque res indubitatam fidem facit,
quòd Philippum filium in hæc loca, tanquam ad bonarum artium
mercaturam, ablegaris. Quem adolescentem, eiúsque diuinam in-

a.ij.   dolem

FIGURE 2.9 Richard Stanyhurst (1547–1618). *Harmonia seu catena dialectica* (London: [For Reginald Wolf], 1570), sig. A1v–A2r. Folger Shelf Mark STC 23229.

We might also think of a Renaissance based in Dublin thanks to Old English travelers and writers. Richard Stanyhurst—Catholic Old English Dubliner, historian, translator, and elegant Latinist—enjoyed the patronage of Lord Deputy Sidney early in his career, and he dedicated his handsomely produced and precociously learned Latin commentary (fig. 2.9) on the ancient Greek philosopher Porphyry to the Lord Deputy. Stanyhurst wrote it while he was a student at Oxford under the tutelage of Edmund Campion, the eventual Catholic martyr, who also visited Sir Henry Sidney in Dublin, in 1570, and wrote a history of Ireland while there (fig. 2.10). In 1577, Stanyhurst wrote a history of Ireland based on Campion's for inclusion in Raphael Holinshed's *Chronicles,* a work groundbreaking for its deliberate promotion of the English language and "nation." His contribution celebrated Old English noble families and their accomplishments.

Not all new ideas and styles came to Dublin via England. Stanyhurst tutored in the household of the cultured Earl of Kildare, who had in his library many books in many languages. In 1582 Stanyhurst published in Leiden a translation of the first four books of Virgil's *Aeneid* into experimental English quantitative meter. Later, in 1584, already in permanent exile, he wrote a defense of Old English claims to power in Ireland, the *De Rebus in Hibernia Gestis,* and his decision to publish in Latin from that point on ensured that his portrayal of Ireland as a discrete society with a "native" elite was accessible to Catholic powers on the Continent.

This, however, was a risky move that smacked of treason—a danger made manifest in the career of the Elizabethan soldier-adventurer Thomas Stukeley, who would prove instrumental in arranging support from continental Catholics for the Desmond uprising of 1569. Stukeley's treachery and the famous circumstances surrounding his death, at the Battle of Alcazar, in 1578, were later played for amusement and staged in London as a cautionary tale in Thomas Heywood's *The Famous Historye of the Life and Death of Captaine Thomas Stukeley* (c. 1596;

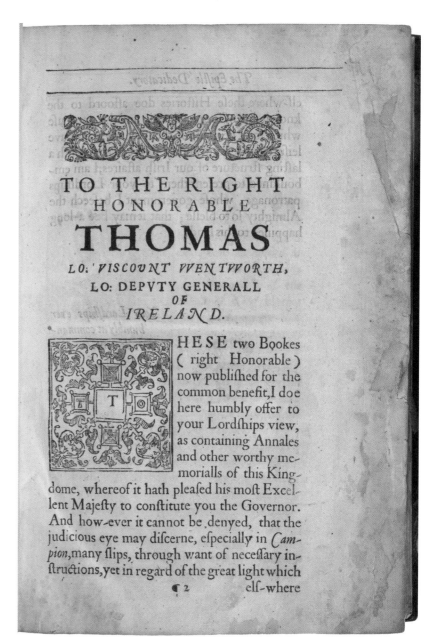

FIGURE 2.10 Edmund Campion (1540–81). *Two histories of Ireland* (Dublin: Societie of Stationers, 1633), preface 2. Folger Shelf Mark STC 25067a copy 1.

19

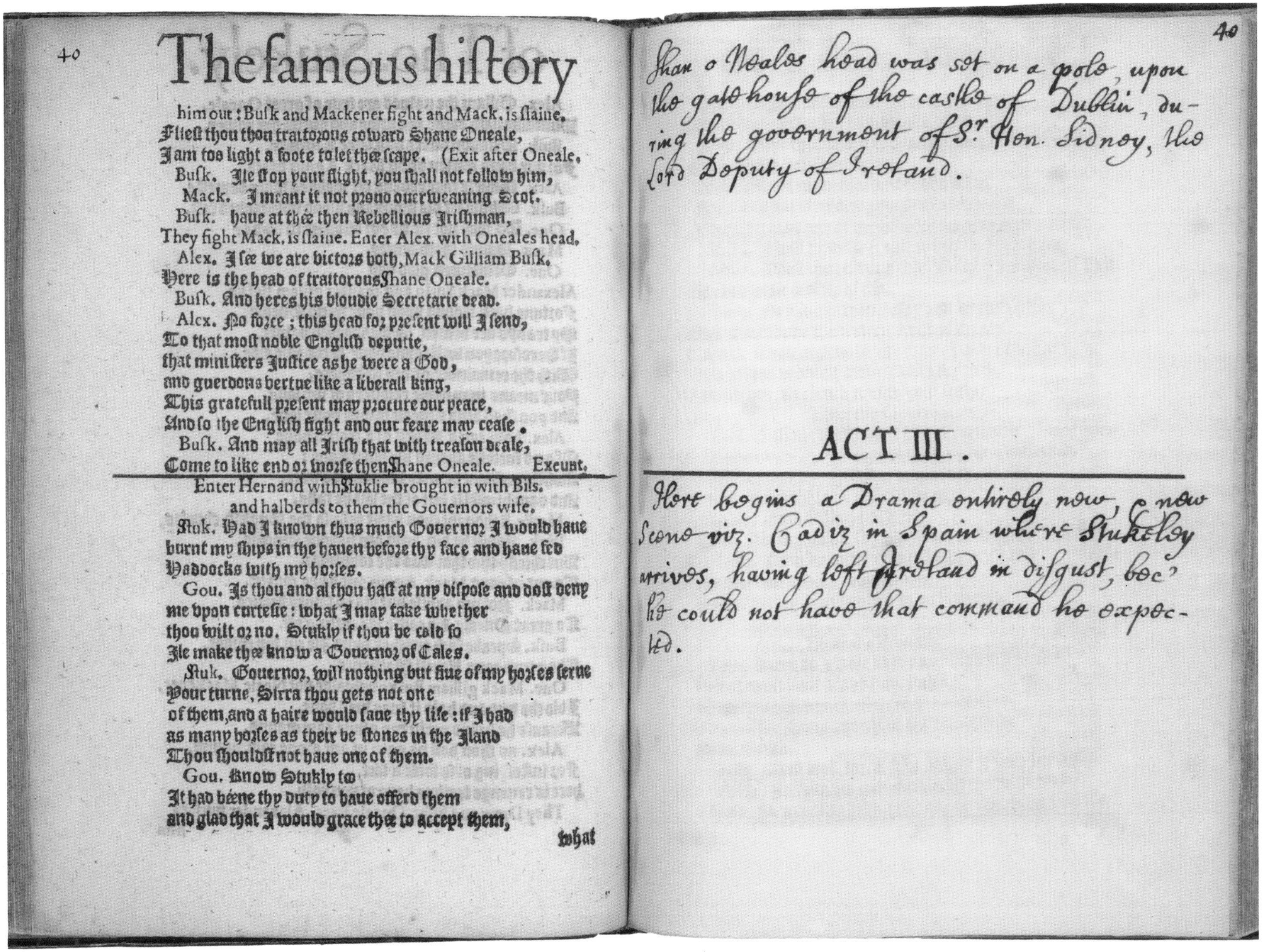

40

The famous history

him out : Busk and Mackener fight and Mack. is flaine.
Fliest thou thou traitorous coward Shane Oneale,
I am too light a foote to let thee scape.   (Exit after Oneale,
   Busk.   Ile stop your flight, you shall not follow him,
   Mack.   I meant it not proud ouertweaning Scot.
   Busk.   haue at thee then Rebellious Irishman,
They fight Mack. is slaine. Enter Alex. with Oneales head,
   Alex.   I see we are victors both, Mack Gilliam Busk.
Here is the head of traitorous Shane Oneale.
   Busk.   And heres his bloudie Secretarie dead.
   Alex.   No force ; this head for present will I send,
To that most noble English deputie,
that ministers Iustice as he were a God,
and guerdons bertue like a liberall king,
This gratefull present may procure our peace,
And so the English fight and our feare may cease .
   Busk.   And may all Irish that with treason deale,
Come to like end or worse then Shane Oneale.   Exeunt.
            Enter Hernand with Stuklie brought in with Bils.
                  and halberds to them the Gouernors wife.
   Ruk.   Had I known thus much Gouernor I would haue
burnt my ships in the hauen before thy face and haue fed
Haddocks with my horses.
   Gou.   Is thou and al thou hast at my dispose and dost deny
me vpon curtesie : what I may take whether
thou wilt or no. Stukly if thou be cold so
Ile make thee know a Gouernor of Cales.
   Ruk.   Gouernor, will nothing but fiue of my horses serue
Your turne, Sirra thou gets not one
of them, and a haire would saue thy life : if I had
as many horses as their be stones in the Iland
Thou shouldst not haue one of them.
   Gou.   Know Stukly to
It had béene thy duty to haue offerd them
and glad that I would grace thee to accept them,
                                                    what

Shan o Neales head was set on a pole, upon the gate house of the castle of Dublin, during the government of Sr. Hen. Sidney, the Lord Deputy of Ireland.

ACT III.

Here begins a Drama entirely new, a new scene viz. Cadiz in Spain where Stukeley arrives, having left Ireland in disgust, bec: he could not have that command he expected.

FIGURE 2.11 *The famous historye of the life and death of Captaine Thomas Stukeley* ([London: William Jaggard], 1605), 40. Folger Shelf Mark STC 23405 copy 2.

published 1605; fig. 2.11). The play is unusual in having a scene set in Ireland, just outside Drogheda, a town on the northern edge of the Pale. In the play, we read of Sir Henry Sidney's great achievements as Lord Deputy. Having killed the great rebel Shane O'Neill, the Irish character Alexander Oge will send O'Neill's head as trophy

> To that most noble English Deputy,
> That ministers justice as he were a god
> And guerdons virtue like a liberal king.
> This grateful present may procure our peace,
> And so the English fight and our fear may cease.[17]

Sidney's rule in Dublin had become famous in London, where Derricke's *Image of Irelande* (fig. 2.12) was also published. Dublin, then, like London was a center of English and Irish interaction. As the power of the Lord Deputy increased, his sharp efforts at reform reached farther out into the Pale and beyond, greatly disturbing the old order.

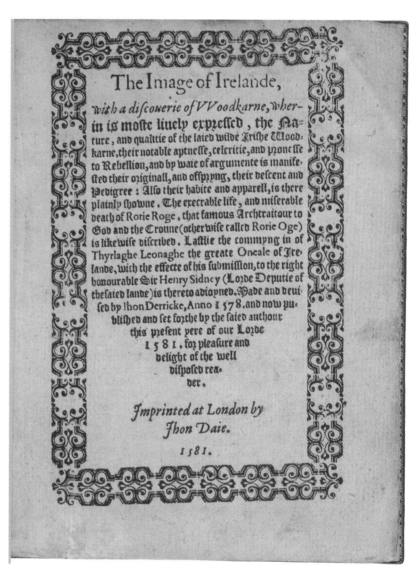

FIGURE 2.12 John Derricke. *The Image of Irelande* (London: [J. Kingston], 1581), title page. Folger Shelf Mark STC 6734.

FIGURE 3.1 John Derricke. *Image of Irelande* (London: [J. Kingston], 1581), plate 11: Rorie Oge, a wild kerne and a defeated rebel, in the forest with wolves for company. Courtesy of the University of Edinburgh.

3
TURMOIL IN THE PALE:
THE DECLINE OF KILDARE

EXTENDING BEYOND DUBLIN was the English Pale, a porous and ill-defined legislative zone created in 1494 for the nominal purpose of protecting Dublin's hinterland from what lay outside it. From its inception, the Pale was a site of cultural hybridity, political negotiation, and occasional rebellion. It contained some of the richest land in Ireland and served as a gateway between country and city, between Gael and *gall* ("foreigner" in Irish, although typically referring to the Anglo-Norman descendants), and indeed among Ireland, England, and the rest of Europe. Contrary to the stereotype of the Pale as a bastion of "English" civility, the Irish language was spoken widely within it during the Tudor-Stuart period.

Most local nobles claimed mixed English-Irish ancestry and were multilingual, speaking and writing English, Irish, Latin, and perhaps some French, Spanish, and Italian. Throughout the sixteenth century, almost all were Catholic; they therefore had to balance their worship, language, and mixed identity with allegiance to the English crown and a state-supported Protestantism, as well as with native Irish powers on their borders.

First and foremost among these Old English nobles were the Fitzgeralds, earls of Kildare, whose seat lay just to the west of Dublin, in Maynooth, County Kildare. During the reign of Henry VII and until the 1530s, successive earls of Kildare served as the English crown's chief governor, or viceroy, in Ireland. They were among the most powerful and wealthy lords in all of England and Ireland. They both

patronized and maintained the peace against minor lords bordering the Pale, many of them Gaelic. Some of these lords, such as the O'Mores of Counties Laois and Offaly (fig. 3.1), grew increasing rebellious after the Kildare lordship fell into crisis.

The family's privileged place at the King's hand would end dramatically with the rebellion of the ninth Earl's son, "Silken Thomas," who took up arms in 1534 to protest his father's fall from favor: a false rumor had reported that his father had been assassinated while in English custody in London. Silken Thomas also protested the crown's preference for "New English" office seekers. Fatefully, he sought to rally support with a cry for "defense of the faith." This raised the stakes considerably: It ensured that no mercy would be coming from the crown, which had already broken from Rome, and launched the theme of religion into traditional English–Irish high politics.

The Kildare rebellion failed miserably and, partly as a result, no Irishman was trusted to hold the post of viceroy until after the Restoration, in 1660. In spite of their fall from monarchical grace, the Kildares would soldier on, still one of the great houses of the realm. Maynooth Castle had a rich library befitting its owners' status and culture, containing works in Latin, French, English, and Irish and covering philosophy, humanism, religion, military tactics, and history. Writers from Cicero to Ovid and from Sir Thomas More to Lorenzo Valla were represented. The Fitzgeralds patronized poetry and prose in English, Latin, and Irish; an ancestor, Gerald Fitzmaurice Fitzgerald,

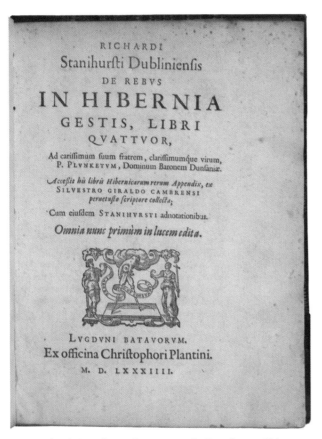

FIGURE 3.2 Richard Stanyhurst (1547–1618). *De rebus in Hibernia gestis . . .* (1584), title page. Folger Shelf Mark DA930.S8 1584 Cage.

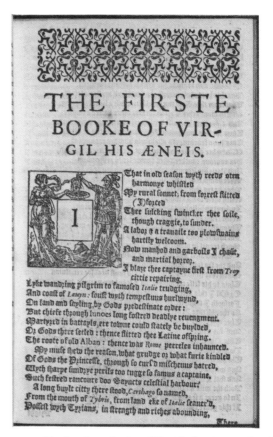

FIGURE 3.3 *The first foure bookes of Virgil's Aeneis, translated into English heroicall verse by Richard Stanyhurst* (London: Henry Bynneman, 1583), sig. A8r. Folger Shelf Mark STC 24807.

a.k.a. Gearóid Iarla, third Earl of Desmond (1338?–98), was himself an accomplished poet in Irish, including courtly love literature.

The august lineage and noble deeds of the Kildares were celebrated by writers of the Pale, such as Richard Stanyhurst (page 19), historian, polemicist, and translator of Virgil who at one time tutored the son and heir of the eleventh, "Wizard" earl—so named for his ability to survive the slings and arrows of court intrigue and maintain his title and head in the dangerous politics of sixteenth-century Ireland. Stanyhurst tes-

tifies to the central place of the house of Kildare in Irish society in both his Irish history, included in Holinshed's *Chronicles,* and his discussion of Irish customs, *De Rebus in Hibernia Gestis* (fig. 3.2).

Two serious repercussions of the rebellion of Silken Thomas were to reinforce the family's continental connections and to harden religious lines between it and the crown. Ireland being a melting pot of Renaissance influences, the Fitzgeralds proudly displayed their continental roots: They claimed ancestry from the Geraldini of Florence.

When forced into exile, in the 1540s, the Wizard Earl of Kildare served as Master of the Horse in the household of Cosimo de' Medici, in Florence, and kept company with the English cardinal in Rome, Reginald Pole. The travels and travails of the stubbornly Catholic Kildares are hinted at in the adventures of the storm-tossed Trojans in Stanyhurst's *Aeneis* (Leiden 1582; London 1583; fig. 3.3), a translation of the first four books of the *Aeneid*. At the opening of the poem, Stanyhurst describes the heroes of the story, the Trojans, as a "martyred" group harassed from on high by the "princess" Juno (who in the allegory would logically stand in for Queen Elizabeth).[18] Stanyhurst, fearing arrest, had himself fled Dublin and London for the Continent in 1580. After the *Aeneis,* he mainly wrote polemical, pro-Catholic pieces in Latin, as well as the *De Rebus* (page 24); became a court alchemist and political adviser to King Philip II of Spain; and was eventually the Jesuit priest of the Hapsburg Archduke of the Netherlands.

The religious tenor of his translation of Virgil is underscored by the illustration of the first, initial capital *I* in the narrative: St. John the Baptist, a martyr, has lost his head to Salome, daughter of the tyrannical king Herod. Catholic-inflected poems and psalms, some addressed in friendly or nostalgic terms to prominent Old English members of the Pale, follow as an appendix to the translation. Best known as an important and bizarre early experiment in quantitative meter, *Aeneis* therefore has a contemporary political message, both consoling and encouraging the harried Old English community of the Pale.

The Italian background of the Fitzgeralds drew comment in London, too. Henry Howard, Earl of Surrey, famously praises the beauty of an Irish lady at the court of Henry VIII, Elizabeth Fitzgerald, a.k.a. the Fair Geraldine (fig. 3.4). In a compliment to her Italian inheritance, Howard refers to her "Tuscan . . . race" and does so in a newfangled art form recently borrowed from Italy and France, that is, the sonnet (see fig. 3.5):

FIGURE 3.4 Master of the Countess of Warwick [attributed]. Portrait of "The Fair Geraldine" Elizabeth Fitzgerald, Countess of Lincoln (c. 1528–90). (England, 16th century), oil on panel. Courtesy of the National Gallery of Ireland.

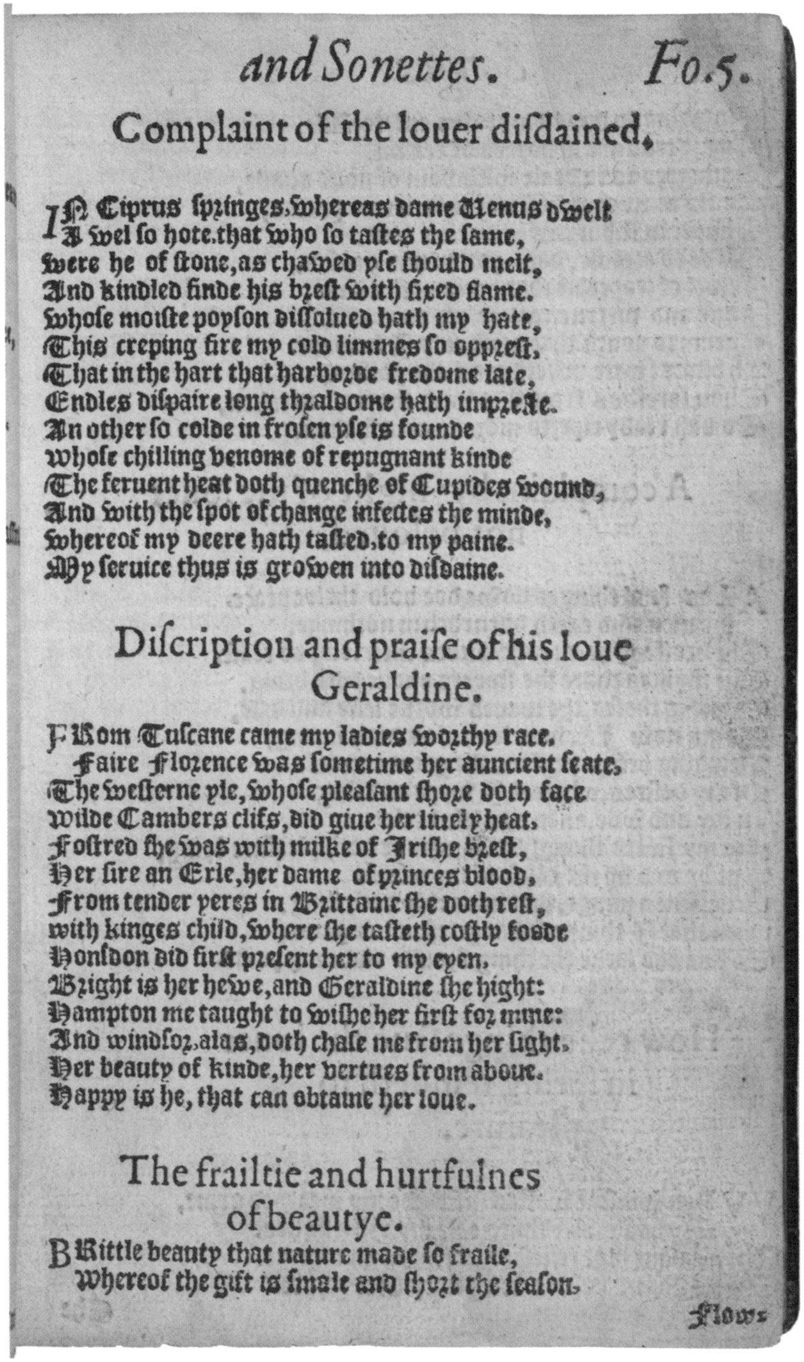

and Sonettes. Fo.5.

Complaint of the louer disdained.

IN Ciprus springes,whereas dame Uenus dwelt
A wel so hote.that who so tastes the same,
Were he of stone,as chawed yse should melt,
And kindled finde his brest with fixed flame,
Whose moiste poyson dissolued hath my hate,
This creping fire my cold limmes so opprest,
That in the hart that harborde fredome late,
Endles dispaire long thraldome hath imprest.
An other so colde in frosen yse is founde
Whose chilling venome of repugnant kinde
The feruent heat doth quenche of Cupides wound,
And with the spot of change infectes the minde.
Whereof my deere hath tasted,to my paine.
My seruice thus is growen into disdaine.

Discription and praise of his loue Geraldine.

FRom Tuscane came my ladies worthy race,
Faire Florence was sometime her auncient seate,
The westerne yle,whose pleasant shore doth face
Wilde Cambers clifs,did giue her liuely heat,
Fostred she was with milke of Irishe brest,
Her sire an Erle,her dame of princes blood,
From tender yeres in Brittaine she doth rest,
with kinges child,where she tasteth costly foode
Honsdon did first present her to my eyen.
Bright is her hewe,and Geraldine she hight:
Hampton me taught to wishe her first for mine:
And windsor,alas,doth chase me from her sight.
Her beauty of kinde,her vertues from aboue.
Happy is he,that can obtaine her loue.

The frailtie and hurtfulnes of beautye.

BRittle beauty that nature made so fraile,
Whereof the gift is smale and short the season.

Flows

From Tuscane came my ladies worthy race,
Fair Florence was sometime her auncient seate,
The westerne yle, whose pleasant shore doth face
Wilde Cambers clifs, did give her lively heat,
Fostred she was with milke of Irishe brest,
Her sire an Erle, her dame of princes blood,
From tender yeres in Brittaine she doth rest
with kinges child, where she tasteth costly foode
Honsdon did first present her to my eyen.
Bright is her hewe, and Geraldine she hight:
Hampton me taught to wishe her first for mine:
And windsor, alas, doth chase me from her sight,
Her beauty of kinde, her vertues from above.
Happy is he, that can obtaine her love.[19]

Irish nobility, therefore, helped set the subject and tone of the English Renaissance. The sonnet's bold spirit of foreign romance fed the imagination of later Tudor writers such as the satirist Thomas Nashe, whose proto-novel *The Unfortunate Traveller* (1594; fig. 3.6) invents the story of Henry Howard meeting the Fair Geraldine in Florence and falling in love. Long before E. M. Forster's novel, a room with a view opened onto County Kildare, not just onto Tuscany and the English countryside.

FIGURE 3.5 Henry Howard, Earl of Surrey (1517?–47). Sonnet to Elizabeth Fitzgerald in *Songes and sonets written by the right honorable Lorde Henry Haward late Earle of Surrey* ([London]: Richard Tottell, 1574), fol. 5r, Folger Shelf Mark STC 13866 copy 1.

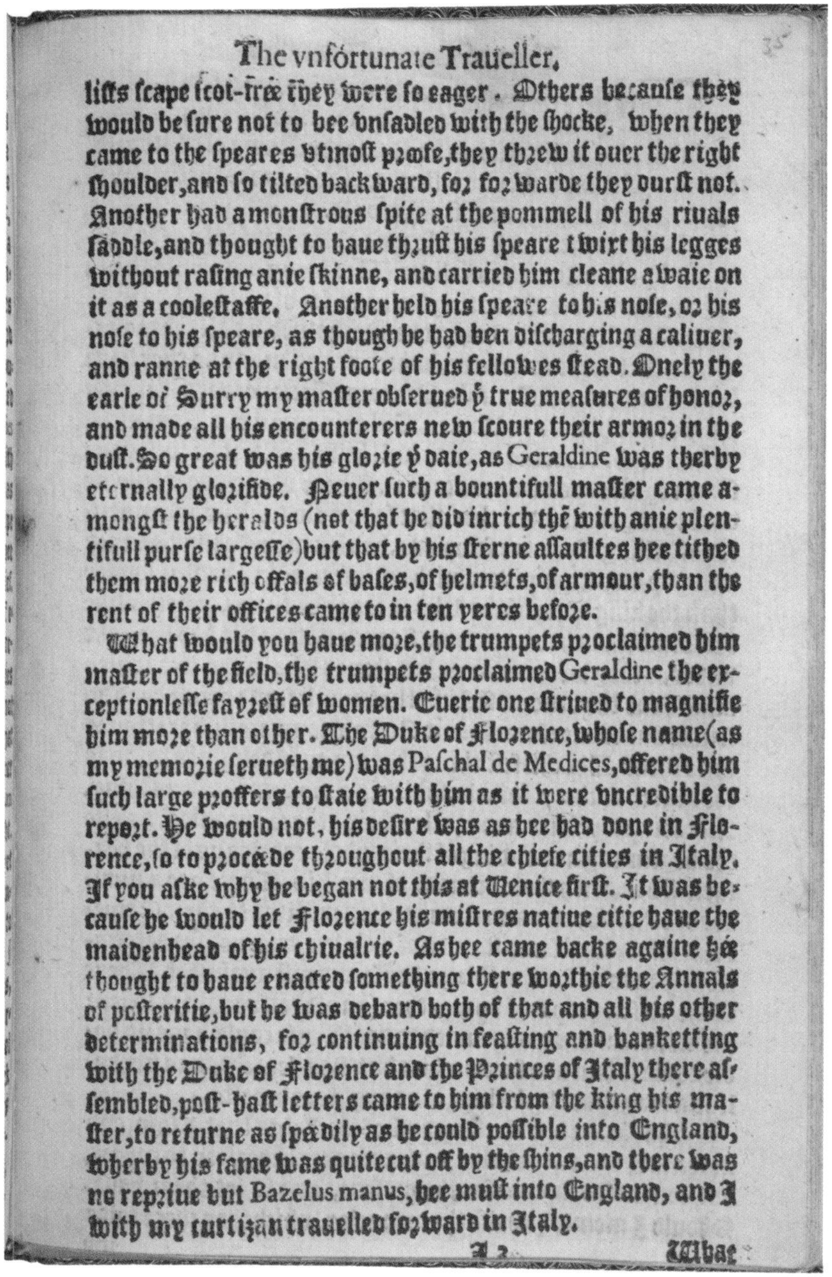

The vnfortunate Traueller.

lifts scape scot-free they were so eager. Others because they would be sure not to bee vnsadled with the shocke, when they came to the speares vtmost proofe, they threw it ouer the right shoulder, and so tilted backward, for forwarde they durst not. Another had a monstrous spite at the pommell of his riuals saddle, and thought to haue thrust his speare twixt his legges without rasing anie skinne, and carried him cleane awaie on it as a coolestaffe. Another held his speare to his nose, or his nose to his speare, as though he had ben discharging a caliuer, and ranne at the right foote of his fellowes stead. Onely the earle of Surry my master obserued the true measures of honor, and made all his encounterers new scoure their armor in the dust. So great was his glorie the daie, as Geraldine was therby eternally glorifide. Neuer such a bountifull master came a-mongst the heralds (not that he did inrich them with anie plen-tifull purse largesse) but that by his sterne assaultes hee tithed them more rich offals of bases, of helmets, of armour, than the rent of their offices came to in ten yeres before.

What would you haue more, the trumpets proclaimed him master of the field, the trumpets proclaimed Geraldine the ex-ceptionlesse fayrest of women. Euerie one striued to magnifie him more than other. The Duke of Florence, whose name (as my memorie serueth me) was Paschal de Medices, offered him such large proffers to staie with him as it were vncredible to report. He would not, his desire was as hee had done in Flo-rence, so to proceade throughout all the chiefe cities in Italy. If you aske why he began not this at Venice first. It was be-cause he would let Florence his mistres natiue citie haue the maidenhead of his chiualrie. As hee came backe againe hee thought to haue enacted something there worthie the Annals of posteritie, but he was debard both of that and all his other determinations, for continuing in feasting and banketting with the Duke of Florence and the Princes of Italy there as-sembled, post-hast letters came to him from the king his ma-ster, to returne as spedily as he could possible into England, wherby his fame was quite cut off by the shins, and there was no repriue but Bazelus manus, hee must into England, and I with my curtizan trauelled forward in Italy.

E 3   What

FIGURE 3.6 Thomas Nashe (1567–1601). *The unfortunate Traveller* (London: T. Scarlet, 1594), 35. Folger Shelf Mark STC 18380.

FIGURE 4.1 Steven van der Meulen (d. 1563 or '64) [attributed]. Portrait of Thomas Butler, tenth Earl of Ormond (1532–1614) (England, 16th century), oil on panel. Courtesy of the National Gallery of Ireland.

4
CONTINUITY AND CHANGE IN LEINSTER:
THE RISE OF ORMOND

Quos casus, quae fata tulit, quibus artibus altum
Conspicuumque decus, nullis delebile monstris
Inuidiae et nullo annorum molimine Thomas,
Ormoniae nactus Satrapas, Mauortius Heros,
Vnigena Aonijs Dea quem nutriuit in antris,
Dicere fert animus.[20]

What fortunes and what fates he bore, and by
What arts the high, conspicuous honor won,
That none of envy's monsters can obscure,
Nor any heavy density of years,
Thomas, the Ormond Satrap, born of Mars,
The Hero, is my spirit fain to sing
Which in the Aonian caves the goddess reared . . .[21]

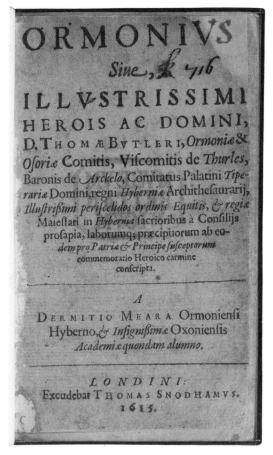

So BEGINS THE VIRGILIAN-STYLE EPIC celebrating the life and heroic deeds of "Black Tom" Butler, tenth Earl of Ormond (1531–1614; fig. 4.1), in Dermot O'Meara's exciting and lengthy *Ormonius* (fig. 4.2). In it we read of Ormond's childhood friendship at court with King Edward VI and of his military support of the crown, including campaigns in England and Scotland on behalf of Queens Mary and Elizabeth. Black Tom also played an active role in advising the government prior to the Battle of Kinsale (see pages 61, 64).

FIGURE 4.2 Dermot O'Meara. *Ormonius* (London: Thomas Snodham, 1615), title page. Folger Shelf Mark STC 17761.

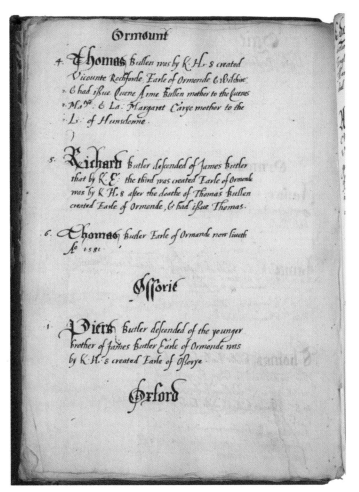

FIGURE 4.3 Genealogies of earls of England and Ireland [manuscript],
1581–c. 1625, Ormount–Oxford. Folger Shelf Mark V.a.266.

(c. 1581; fig. 4.3) graphically makes this point. This list of "earls of England and Ireland" makes no distinctions between English and Irish titles. The Earls of Ormond and Ossory (both titles held by the Butlers) are placed alphabetically with their peers residing in England; they are followed by the Earls of Oxford, one of England's great lines. The "Englishness" of the Ormond title and its importance to the crown are also manifest in the person noted at the top of the page: Thomas Bullen (Boleyn). In his pursuit of Anne Boleyn, Henry VIII granted the ancient title to her father. As noted here, the holder of the Ormond lordship traditionally held the title Earl of Wiltshire in England. On Boleyn's fall from grace, the titles reverted back to the Butlers, who once again enjoyed lands and peerage titles in Ireland and England.

Ormond's fortunes demonstrate dramatically that the experience of the Old English nobility was not uniform under the Tudors. As their rivals the Kildares fell from grace (and their southern rivals the earls of Desmond too; see chapter 5), so the Butler house of Ormond rose to fill the place of the crown's local favorite. It is not true, therefore, that only English newcomers profited from Irish rebellion. Some of the Butlers also resettled during this period: The earl's brothers in Tipperary, less favored by the crown and hence less insulated from the New English challenge, took up arms against the government in 1569. But the earl himself was staunchly loyal and further cemented his connection to Elizabeth's regime by helping to suppress his rebellious brethren.

A man of great wealth, connection, and diplomatic skill across ethnic lines, Ormond was secure enough in his relationship to the crown to be allowed to govern his territories as the last remaining lord palatine in the Tudor realms. Although subordinate to the monarchy and its laws, the earl was able to pursue his own legal and economic prerogatives locally. This caused much friction among envious rivals, English and Irish alike.

Published in London in 1615, the year after the earl's death, in County Tipperary, it advertises the fame of Ormond in the hope that his house and heirs would continue to benefit during the Stuart regime from the extraordinary power and prestige conferred upon him by the English court, especially by his cousin Queen Elizabeth I during her reign (1558–1603). It is important to remember that Ormond was an English noble living in Ireland. An alphabetical list of Tudor aristocrats

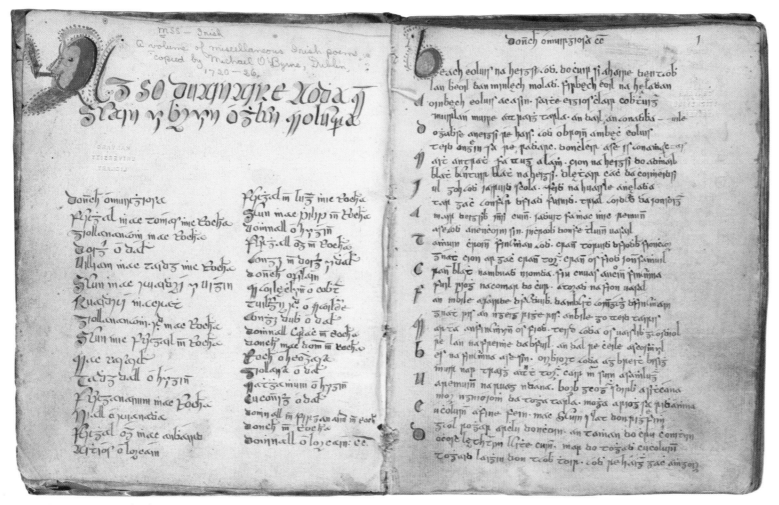

FIGURE 4.4 Michael O'Byrne (18th century). *Ag so Duainaire Aodha mac Seain Ui Bhruin ó Glen Moluara* [manuscript] (1726–28), fol. 1.
Courtesy of Harvard University Library, Shelf Mark MS Ir6.

31

The earl had numerous, and powerful, Gaelic noble lineages as neighbors, among them the O'Kennedys, the O'Mores, the Kavanaghs, the O'Tooles, and the O'Byrnes. Their connections to the crown were not unlike those of their Old English neighbors: Loyalty and rebellion were always options, choices being made according to circumstance and, frequently, interpersonal relations.

The *duanaire,* or poem book (fig. 4.4), of the Wicklow O'Byrnes consists largely of eulogistic verses and genealogical records of that family. Richly literary and highly formalized, court poems such as these were not compiled mainly for aesthetic purposes, as were English anthologies. Rather, they were more akin to "state papers": records of battles, family lines, and political advice. The typical English word

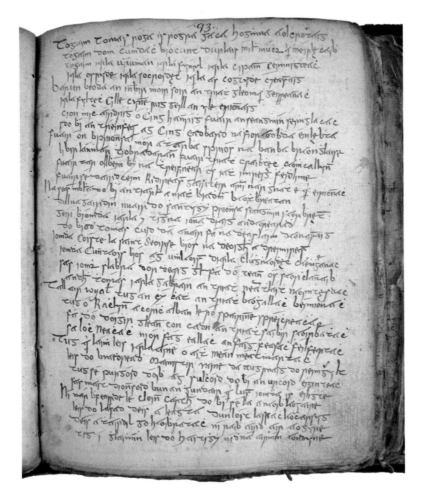

FIGURE 4.5 Mícheál mac Peadair Uí Longáin, scribe. Miscellany [manuscript], 18th century, 93: "Toghaim Tomás rógha" on Black Thomas Butler, Earl of Ormond. Courtesy of the Royal Irish Academy, Shelf Mark MS 23 N 15.

the *ollúna* (plural of *ollamh*) could also push and critique their lords and patrons.

Every Gaelic lineage would have kept a *duanaire,* though few survive; the poem book pictured here is in fact an early-eighteenth-century copy of a now lost original. This stunning collection opens with a list on the left of the poets whose work appears and on the right the first verse is a praise poem to Aodh O'Byrne by Donnchad Ó Muirgiosa. The poems were written during most of the sixteenth century, and chronicle the efforts of an ancient Gaelic lineage to maintain its power and place in a new world of a centralizing and expansionist crown.

Irish poets were also patronized by Old English earls. In an anonymous poem to "Black Tom" Butler, the tenth Earl (also Viscount Thurles), the poet presents himself as chief bard to the mighty nobleman (fig. 4.5):

> *Toghaim Tomas, rogha's ró-ghrádh,*
> *Gacha h-óg-mhná aol-chrothaigh;*
> *Toghaim dam chúmhdach biocunt Dúrlais,*
> *Míleadh múchda ar mhéirliocaibh.*

> My choice is Thomas, the choice and true love
> Of every fair-skinned young maiden;
> I select as my patron the Viscount Thurles,
> The chieftain who annihilates rebels.[22]

used to describe their authors—*bard*—does their position little justice and obscures the fundamental political and social role they played. Bards were nobles in their own right, with the same "honor price" as had secular lords according to Brehon (that is, Irish) law. Indeed, one could not be a Gaelic head of a lordship without having a chief poet, or *ollamh filíochta,* to provide legitimacy and advice. No mere yes-men,

This praise for the earl's martial qualities is echoed by another Irishman, the physician-cum-poet O'Meara quoted at the beginning of this chapter, and also by the Englishman Thomas Churchyard, whose *A Scourge for Rebels* (1584; fig. 4.6) praised Ormond's part in quelling the great Desmond rebellion (1579–83), where he was general of the Queen's armies in Munster. The anonymous verse then goes on to praise the earl's wife, the Englishwoman Elizabeth Sheffield, for her

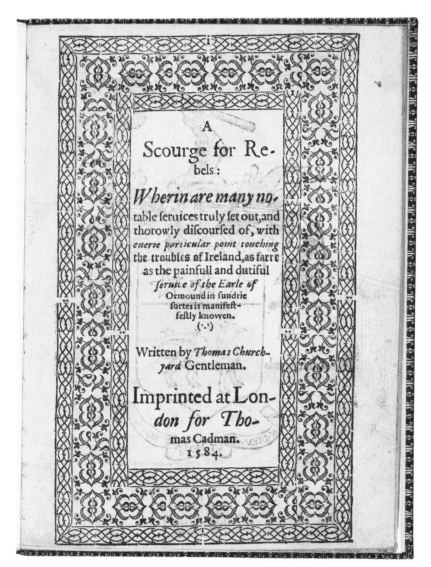

FIGURE 4.6 Thomas Churchyard (1520?–1604). *A Scourge for Rebels* (London: [Thomas Dawson], 1584), title page and Churchyard's coat of arms. Courtesy of Huntington Library Shelf Mark 56400.

beauty, manner, and education, and their mansion at Carrick-on-Suir in Tipperary as a site of noble hospitality and cosmopolitan sensibili-ties. Here again the poet was not alone in his theme, for it bears a strik-ing resemblance to the dedicatory sonnet to the tenth Earl appended

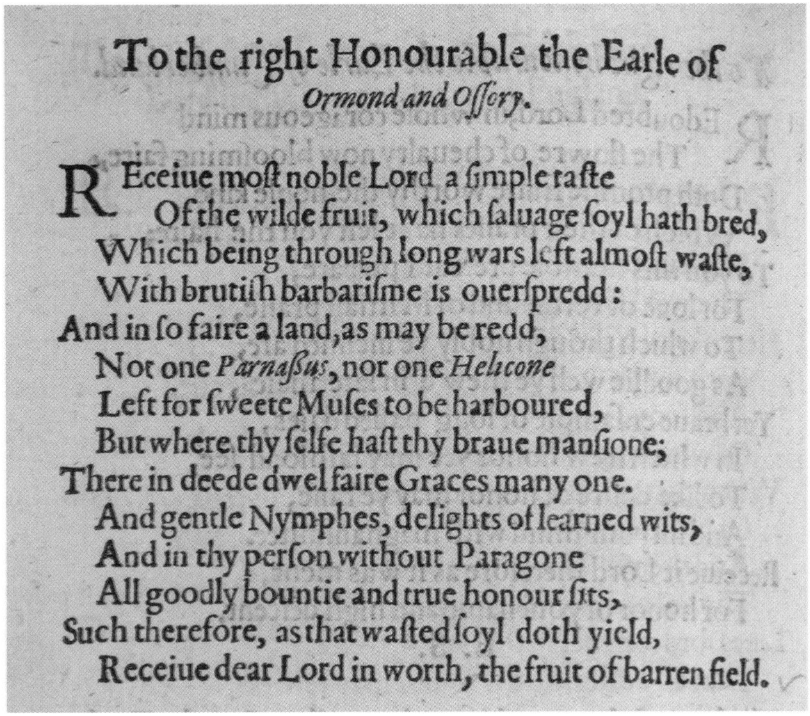

To the right Honourable the Earle of
Ormond and Ossory.

Receiue most noble Lord a simple taste
  Of the wilde fruit, which saluage soyl hath bred,
Which being through long wars left almost waste,
With brutish barbarisme is ouerspredd:
And in so faire a land, as may be redd,
Not one *Parnassus*, nor one *Helicone*
Left for sweete Muses to be harboured,
But where thy selfe hast thy braue mansione;
There in deede dwel faire Graces many one.
  And gentle Nymphes, delights of learned wits,
  And in thy person without Paragone
All goodly bountie and true honour sits,
Such therefore, as that wasted soyl doth yield,
  Receiue dear Lord in worth, the fruit of barren field.

FIGURE 4.7 Edmund Spenser (1552?–1599). *The faerie queene* (London: [John Wolfe], 1590), detail from sig. 2Q2v–2Q2r, Folger Shelf Mark STC 23080.

FIGURE 4.8 Plaster cast made from portrait in relief (1565–75) of Queen Elizabeth I from the ornamental frieze of the Long Gallery, Ormond Castle, Carrick-On-Suir, County Tipperary, Ireland. Courtesy of the National Monument Service, Office of Public Works, Ireland.

to the 1590 edition of Edmund Spenser's *The Faerie Queene* (fig. 4.7). The sonnet praises the earl's "mansion" (which could also have been his castle in Kilkenny) where dwell "faire Graces many one."[23]

This was no mere flattery, as the tenth Earl stands out as an extraordinary figure for his refined tastes in English, Irish, and Latin culture and letters, and for his proximity to the English court, where he spent much of his life. There is perhaps no better sign of his integration into the monarchical inner circle than the anonymous libel *Leycesters Commonwealth* (fig. 4.9). This scurrilous attack on the deeds and reputation of the Queen's favorite, the Earl of Leicester, was published on the Continent but widely circulated in England. Among the sinful

misdeeds of Leicester, claimed the unknown author, was that he attempted to poison Ormond. One way for the writer to slander Leicester was to demonstrate his murderous designs on those cherished by the Queen. And she cherished Black Tom in part as a matter of blood and faith: He was her cousin through the Boleyn family, a Protestant (although he converted to Catholicism on his deathbed), and close to her half brother Edward VI in his youth. Indeed, plaster busts of both monarchs, alternating with the allegorical figures of Justice and Equity, line the great hall of Ormond's fully restored Elizabethan mansion at Carrick-on-Suir (fig. 4.8). Ormond was a hero and an enemy on a grand stage.

But as among manie, none vvere more odious &
misliked of all men, then thofe againſt Monſieur
Simiers a ſtraunger & Ambaſſador: vvhom firſt he
practiſed to haue poyſoned (as hath bene touched

The inté
ded mur-
der of Mõ
ſieur Si-
miers by
ſundrye
meanes.

before) & vvhen that deuiſe toke not place, thẽ he
appointed that Robin Tider his man(as after vpon
his ale bench he confeſſed) ſhould haue ſlaine him
at the blacke friars at Grenevvich as he vvent furth
at the garden gate: but miſſing alſo of that purpoſe,
for that he found the Gentleman better prouided
and guarded then he expected, he delt vvyth certai-
ne Fluſſhyners and other Pyrates to ſinke him at
ſea vvyth the Engliſhe Gentlemen his fauourers,
that accompanied him at his returne into Fraunce.
And though they miſſed of this practize alſo, (as
not daring to ſet vpon him for feare of ſome of her
Ma. ſhippes, vvho, to break of this deſignement at-
tended by ſpecial commaundement, to vvaſte him
ouer in ſafitie) yet the foreſaid Engliſh Gentlemẽ,
vvere holden fovver hovvers in chaſe at their
comming backe: as M. Ravvley vvel knovvveth
being then preſent, and tvvo of the Chacers named
Clark and Harris confeſſed aftervvard the vvhole
deſignement.

The Earle of Ormond in like vvyſe hath of-

The inté-
ded mur-
der of the
Earle of
Ormond.

ten declared, and vvill auovvch it to my Lord
of Leyceſters face, vvhen ſo euer he ſhalbe called to the ſame, that at ſuch tyme as this man
had a quarell vvyth him and therby vvas like-
lie to be enforcede to the fielde (vvhiche he
trembled to thinke of) he firſt ſoughte by all
meanes to get him made avvay by ſecret mur-

der, offeringe fiue hundreth poundes for the
doing therof : and ſecondlie vvhen that deuiſe
toke no place, he appointed vvyth him the
fielde, but Secretlie ſuborning his ſeruaunte
vvyllm Killegre to lye in the vvaye vvhere VVyllm
Killegre
Ormonde ſhoulde paſſe, and ſo to maſſaker him
vvyth a Calliuer, before he came to the place
appointed. VVhich murder thoughe it toke no
effecte, for that the matter vvas taken vp, before the day of meetinge : yet vvas Killigre placed aftervvarde in her Ma. Priuie Chamber by
Leyceſter, for ſhevving his redie minde, to do
for his maſter ſo faythful a ſeruice.

So faithfull a ſeruice (quoth I ?) truelie, in
my opinion, it vvas but an vnfit preferment, SCHOL.
for ſo facinorous a facte. And as I vvoulde be
lothe that manie of his Italians, or other of that
arte, ſhoulde come nighe aboute her Ma. kitchen: ſo muche leſſe vvould I, that manie ſuche
his bloodie Champions, ſhoulde be placed by
him in her highneſſe chamber. Albeit for this
Gentleman in particulare, it may be, that vvyth
chaunge of his place in ſeruice, he hath chaun-
ged alſo his minde and affection, and recey-
ued better inſtruction in the feare of the
Lorde.

But yet in generall I muſte needes ſay, that it
cannot be but preiudicial & exceeding daungerous
vnto our noble Prince and Realm, that anie one
mã vvhatſoeuer(eſpecialie ſuch a one as the vvorld
taketh this man to be) ſhould grovv to ſo abſo-
lute authoritie and commaundrie in the Court, as

35

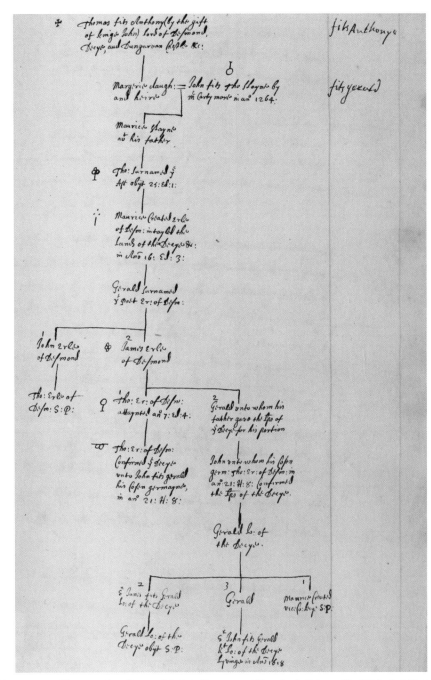

FIGURE 5.1 Desmond pedigree, fol. 86. Courtesy of Lambeth Palace, Shelf Mark MS 610.

5
fall of a munster earldom: the destruction of desmond

THE EARL OF ORMOND'S GREAT RIVAL for power in the south-western province of Munster was the Earl of Desmond (fig. 5.1), a Fitzgerald cousin of the earls of Kildare. A poem in Latin, "Eterne Deus," preached from the altar in 1381 by Richard, Bishop of Cloyne, in County Cork, lamented "Eterne Deus, / duo sunt in Momonia / qui destruunt nos / et bona nostra" (Eternal God, / there are two in Munster / who destroy us / and what is ours), and predicted their downfall: "in the end / the Lord will destroy [them] / through Christ, our Lord. / Amen."[24] Richard was immediately fired from his post, but his prophecy would come true.

Like Ormond and Kildare, the house of Desmond had a long, wealthy, and proud history in Ireland dating back to the Anglo-Norman conquest. The earldom also influenced English politics, as when the ninth Earl supported the Perkin Warbeck invasion (see pages 6–7). Unlike the Kildare branch of the family, which sur-vived the Tudors (albeit by 1600 much diminished), Desmond and his heirs recovered virtually nothing after their disastrous rebellion was finally crushed, in 1583. The fifteenth, "Rebel" Earl, Gerald Fitzgerald, was hunted down and decapitated in a dark Kerry glen and the attain-der (crown seizure on grounds of treason) of his property and that of his associates followed. His heir, the so-called Tower Earl, endured long prison spells in London, and despite a brief, attempted restoration with crown backing in 1600, he died in the capital a year later, in debt and shunned by his monarch.

On display here is the Tower Earl's copy of the poetry of Petrarch, *Le Volgari Opere del Petrarcha con la Espositione di Alessandro Vellutello da Lucca* (Venice 1525; see fig. 5.2). Desmond inscribed and annotated the book in three languages: English, French, and Italian. His warm dedication to his jail keeper, Beaupre Bell, governor of the Tower, can be seen as a heart-wrenching example of Stockholm syndrome: He signs the title page to his "beloved friend" Bell, adding the motto "Not as I would but as I am." The motto indicates his integrity but also, sadly, emphasizes his state as a perpetual prisoner.

From being one of the wealthiest and most powerful earldoms in England and Ireland in the mid-sixteenth century, by the early seven-teenth century the Desmond title had become impotent and was passed into the hands of one of King James's Scottish favorites: Richard Preston, Lord Dingwall, who was granted the title in 1619. Continu-ance of the family's fortunes in Ireland would be left to the Tower Earl's irrepressible mother, Eleanor, Countess of Desmond. A skillful

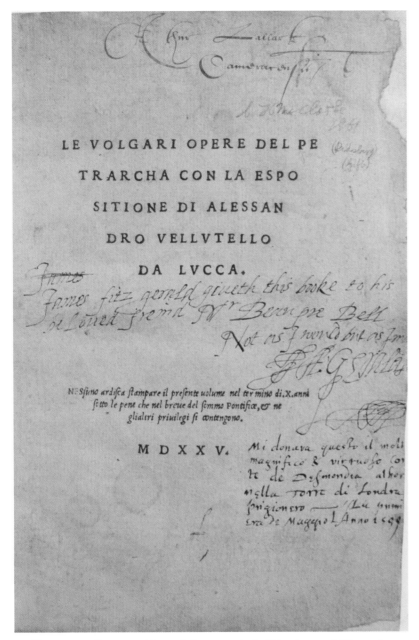

FIGURE 5.2 Francesco Petrarch (1304–74). *Le Volgari opere del Petrarcha con la espositione di Alessandro Vellutello da Lucca* (Venice, 1525), title page. Courtesy of Rolf and Magda Loeber.

diplomat, Eleanor in 1597 remarried Donogh O'Connor, the Gaelic Lord of Sligo (d. 1609), and prospered in London and Connacht until her death (c. 1638).

Often seen as the most "Gaelicized" of the three great Old English earls (Ormond, Desmond, and Kildare), and certainly the most geographically distant from Dublin, the Desmonds enjoyed little more favor with the crown under Elizabeth I than they did during their days backing Warbeck. This was not helped by their staunch Catholicism. Nevertheless, they were not incapable of alliance and negotiation with crown representatives. The fifteenth earl, for example, was an ally of subsequent Sussex and Sidney Lord Deputyships and factions at court in the 1550s and '60s.

Eventually, however, his influence in London weakened just as that of Ormond grew. In 1569, while the fifteenth earl and his brother John were in prison, an abortive rebellion was launched in his territory by one of his captains and close allies, James Fitzmaurice Fitzgerald. In the 1570s, Desmond continued to be pushed and prodded at home by aggressive local officials aiming to curb his powers and liberties. His own descent into open rebellion, commencing in 1579, caused far greater carnage and suffering than did that of James Fitzmaurice, or that of Silken Thomas of Kildare in the mid-1530s. The Kildare uprising spoke the language of defense of the Catholic faith, but the Desmond offensive marked the true flowering of an ideology of "faith and fatherland" in the country. Among other notable events, a pro-Catholic revolt led by Viscount Baltinglass was launched simultaneously in the Dublin Pale, and in Munster, James Fitzmaurice Fitzgerald returned from continental exile and brought with him soldiers, money, and papal support in an effort to overthrow Elizabeth's authority.

The prolific, if purple, pen of Thomas Churchyard (see page 32) describes the perils of warfare in Munster in his aptly titled *The Miserie of Flaunders . . . and Unquietnes of Ireland* (1579; fig. 5.3). Churchyard

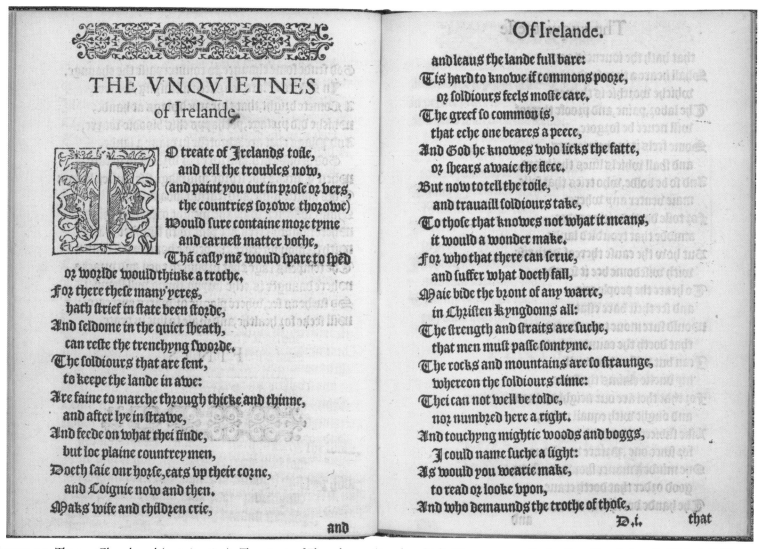

THE VNQVIETNES
of Irelande.

TO treate of Irelands toile,
    and tell the troubles now,
(and paint you out in prose oz vers,
    the countries sozowe thozowe)
Would sure containe moze tyme
    and earnest matter bothe,
      Thā easly mē would spare to sped
oz wozlde would thinke a trothe.
Foz there these many yeres,
    hath strief in state been stozde,
And seldome in the quiet sheath,
    can reste the trenchyng swozde.
The soldiours that are sent,
    to keepe the lande in awe:
Are faine to marche thzough thicke and thinne,
    and after lye in strawe,
And feede on what thei finde,
    but loe plaine countrey men,
Doeth saie our hozse, eats vp their cozne,
    and Coignie now and then.
Maks wife and childzen crie,

                and

Of Irelande.

and leaus the lande full bare:
Tis hard to knowe if commons pooze,
    oz soldiours feels moste care.
The greef so commou is,
    that eche one beares a peece,
And God he knowes who licks the fatte,
    oz shears awaie the flece.
But now to tell the toile,
    and trauaill soldiours take,
To those that knowes not what it means,
    it would a wonder make.
Foz who that there can serue,
    and suffer what doeth fall,
Maie bide the bzont of any warre,
    in Chzisten kyngdoms all:
The strength and straits are suche,
    that men must passe somtyme.
The rocks and mountains are so straunge,
    whereon the soldiours clime:
Thei can not well be tolde,
    noz numbzed here a right.
And touchyng mightie woods and boggs,
    I could name suche a sight:
As would you wearie make,
    to read oz looke vpon,
And who demaunds the trothe of those,
              D.i.   **that**

FIGURE 5.3 Thomas Churchyard (1520?–1604). *The miserie of Flaunders . . .* (London: [Felix Kingston, 1579]), sig. C3v–D1r. Folger Shelf Mark STC 5243.

was a soldier and thus knew of what he wrote; the work, in fact, is curious for its celebration of the rank and file. He was also a propagandist, however, and a seeker of patronage who lauded the deeds of the Earl of Ormond. Churchyard pushed a decidedly pro-government view of events against Desmond—events he situated within a pan-European context of revolts and rebellions that inevitably drew in the English and, thus, served to increase their power on land and sea.

Edmund Spenser's *View of the Present State of Ireland* (c. 1596;

FIGURE 5.4 [Anthony Munday?]. *The true reporte of the prosperous successe which God gave unto our English Souldiours* (London: Edward White, 1581), title page. Courtesy of Cambridge University Library.

published 1633) contains the best-known description of the famine wrought by the Desmond rebellion on the innocent and the guilty alike:

> Ere one year and a half they were brought to such retchedness as that any stony heart would have rued the same. Out of every corner of the woods and glens they came creeping forth upon their hands, for their legs could not bear them; they looked like anatomies of death, they spake like ghosts, crying out of their graves. They did eat of the dead carrions, happy were they if they could find them, yea, and one another soon after, insomuch as the very carcasses they spared not to scrape out of their graves; and if they found a plot of water-cresses or shamrocks, there they flocked as to a feast for the time, yet not able long to continue there withal; that in short space there were none almost left, and a most populous and plentiful country suddenly made void of man or beast. Yet sure in all that war, there perished not many by the sword, but all by the extremity of famine which they themselves had wrought.[25]

Spenser's mouthpiece, Irenius, conveys the full horrors of the war, including cannibalism. The concluding sentence, however, blames it all squarely on the obstinate behavior of the Irish rebels themselves.

Out of the bloody crucible of the Desmond rebellion were shaped many reputations, villains and heroes who each felt that God was on his or her side. A breathless, Bible-thumping narrative of events by the mysterious "A.M." (perhaps Anthony Munday), *The True Reporte of the Prosperous Success which God Gave unto our English Souldiours* (1581; fig. 5.4), celebrates the "godly" victory of crown forces against Fitzmaurice's invading papal expeditionary force at Smerwick Fort, County Kerry, in 1580.

After a three-day siege in an isolated promontory fort overlooking an Atlantic cliff, bombarded by crown artillery, the invaders, more than five hundred mostly Italian and some Spanish soldiers, gave their unconditional surrender. The Earl of Desmond, whose rebellion they had traveled so far to support, had failed to show up to relieve them. The crown forces, led by the Lord Deputy of Ireland, Arthur, Lord Grey de Wilton, massacred all but a small number of the officers, and these were kept for ransom. A few unfortunate Irish among them, including a woman and a priest, were tortured before being killed.

Grey was Spenser's employer in Ireland and earns high praise for his actions in the poet's *View*—a combination history, ethnography, and policy tract. Spenser lauds the Deputy's religious (Protestant) zeal and aggressive approach to suppressing the rebellion, including at Smerwick. Many on the Irish side, not surprisingly, took the opposite stance, and the event is still regarded as a prime example of English treachery. Grey's own employer, Queen Elizabeth I, recalled him in 1582, more for his failure to control Irish finances than for any perceived excesses at Smerwick; he was also eager to quit this post. In the end, it was the more conciliatory and pragmatic Thomas Butler, tenth Earl of Ormond, who oversaw the rebellion's end.

Although Grey's reputation was sullied by events in Ireland, another one took spectacular flight. Among the besiegers of Smerwick Fort was the young captain Walter Raleigh. Raleigh, the famous author and explorer, advised the Queen on Irish matters and was one of the principal newcomers to divide the Desmond spoils. Raleigh's good looks, intelligence, political acumen, and heroic military exploits in Ireland and elsewhere earned him a knighthood and attention at court, where in the 1580s he rose as the Queen's favorite. His many deeds in Ireland (including his role in the Smerwick massacre) are celebrated in John Hooker's triumphal, pro-Protestant Irish history, contained in the second edition (1586) of Holinshed's *Chronicles* (see fig. 5.5).

More than one spotlight shone on Raleigh's actions in Ireland. Episodes in Hooker that lauded his heroism are reflected in Book III of Spenser's 1596 romance epic *The Faerie Queene* (see fig. 5.6), another Protestant "history" that, like Hooker's chronicle, is dedicated in part to Raleigh and is preoccupied with the struggle in Ireland, albeit hidden within the many shadows of its allegorical method. Here Raleigh is allegorized as Spenser's character Timias (a "gentle Squire"), who fights off a treacherous ambush at a ford. Timias is attacked by three suspiciously Irish-looking "fosters," or villains:

> Anone one sent out of the thicket neare
> A cruell shaft [arrow], headed with deadly ill,
> And fethered with an unlucky quill;
> The wicked steele stayd not, till it did light
> In his [Timias's] left thigh, and deepely did it thrill:
> Exceeding griefe that wound in him empight,
> But more that with his foes he could not come to fight.
>
> At last through wrath and vengeaunce making way,
> He on the bancke arriv'd with mickle paine,
> Where the third brother him did sore assay,
> And drove at him with all his might and maine
> A forrest bill, which both his hands did straine;
> But warily he did avoide the blow,
> And with his speare requited him [the foster] againe,
> That both his sides were thrilled with the throw,
> And a large streame of bloud out of the wound did flow.
>
> He tombling downe, with gnashing teeth did bite
> The bitter earth, and bad to let him in
> Into the balefull house of endlesse night,
> Where wicked ghosts do waile their former sin . . .[26]

Not only did Raleigh win real battles against the "sinning" Irish during the Desmond rebellion, but he was subsequently on the ground in London to win a large piece of the plantation that followed.

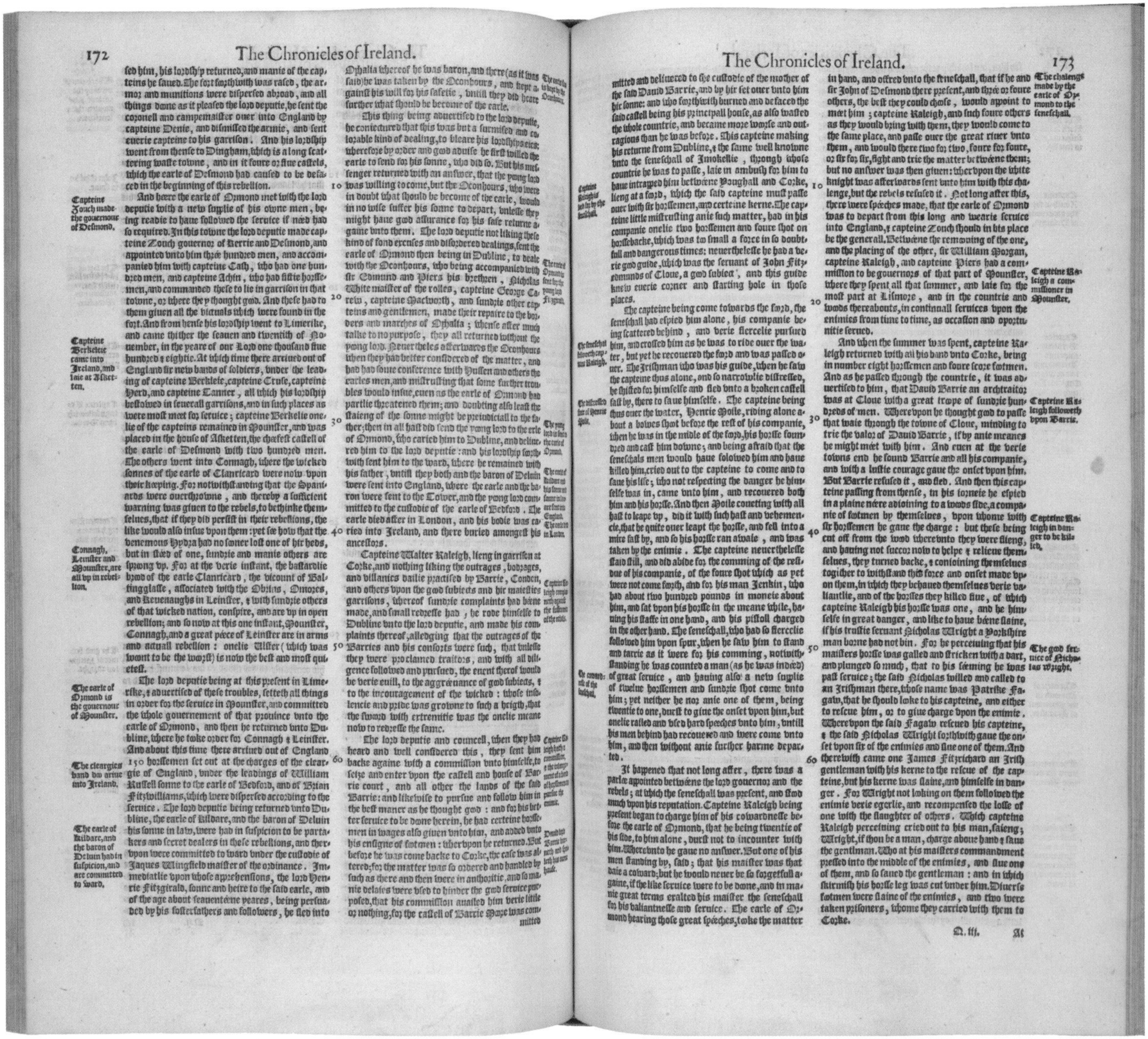

FIGURE 5.5 Raphael Holinshed (d. 1580?). *Chronicles of England, Scotlande, and Irelande* ([London: Henry Denham, 1587]), 172–73, Folger Shelf Mark STC 13569 copy 2 v.1.

Nathlesse the villen sped himselfe so well,
    Whether through swiftnesse of his speedy beast,
    Or knowledge of those woods, where he did dwell,
    That shortly he from daunger was releast,
    And out of sight escaped at the least;
    Yet not escaped from the dew reward
    Of his bad deeds, which dayly he increast,
    Ne ceased not, till him oppressed hard
The heauy plague, that for such leachours is prepard.

For soone as he was vanisht out of sight,
    His coward courage gan emboldned bee,
    And cast t'auenge him of that fowle despight,
    Which he had borne of his bold enimee.
    Tho to his brethren came: for they were three
    Vngratious children of one gracelesse sire,
    And vnto them complained, how that he
    Had vsed bene of that foolehardy Squire;
So them with bitter words he stird to bloudy ire.

Forthwith themselues with their sad instruments
    Of spoyle and murder they gan arme byliue,
    And with him forth into the forest went,
    To wreake the wrath, which he did earst reuiue
    In their sterne brests, on him which late did driue
    Their brother to reproch and shamefull flight :
    For they had vow'd, that neuer he aliue
    Out of that forest should escape their might;
Vile rancour their rude harts had fild with such despight.

Within that wood there was a couert glade,
    Foreby a narrow foord, to them well knowne,
    Through which it was vneath for wight to wade;
    And now by fortune it was ouerflowne:

By that same way they knew that Squire vnknowne
    Mote algates passe; for thy themselues they set
    There in await, with thicke woods ouer growne,
    And all the while their malice they did whet
With cruell threats, his passage through the ford to let.

It fortuned, as they deuized had,
    The gentle Squire came ryding that same way,
    Vnweeting of their wile and treason bad,
    And through the ford to passen did assay;
    But that fierce foster, which late fled away,
    Stoutly forth stepping on the further shore,
    Him boldly bad his passage there to stay,
    Till he had made amends, and full restore
For all the damage, which he had him doen afore.

With that at him a quiu'ring dart he threw,
    With so fell force and villeinous despighte,
    That through his haberieon the forkehead flew,
    And through the linked mayles empierced quite,
    But had no powre in his soft flesh to bite :
    That stroke the hardy Squire did sore displease,
    But more that him he could not come to smite;
    For by no meanes the high banke he could sease,
But labour'd long in that deepe ford with vaine disease.

And still the foster with his long bore-speare
    Him kept from landing at his wished will;
    Anone one sent out of the thicket neare
    A cruell shaft, headed with deadly ill,
    And fethered with an vnlucky quill;
    The wicked steele stayd not, till it did light
    In his left thigh, and deepely did it thrill:
    Exceeding griefe that wound in him empight,
But more that with his foes he could not come to fight.

FIGURE 5.6 Edmund Spenser (1552?–99). *The faerie queene* (London: [Richard Field], 1596), 466–67. Folger Shelf Mark STC 23082 copy 2 v.1.

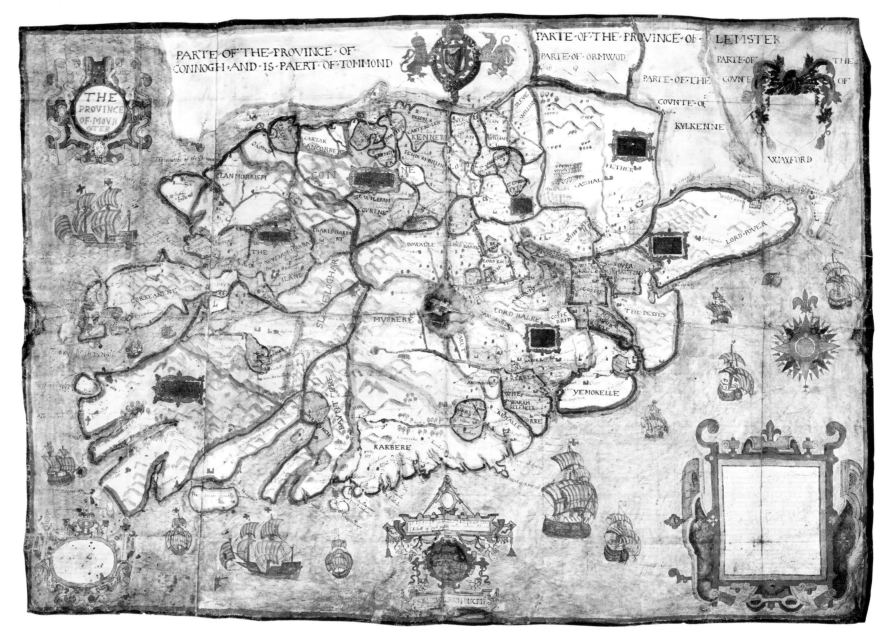

PARTE·OF·THE·PROVINCE·OF·CONNOGH·AND·IS·PAERT·OF·TOMMOND

PARTE·OF·THE·PROVINCE·OF·LEIMSTER

PARTE·OF·ORMWOD

PARTE·OF·THE·COVNTE·OF

COVNTE·OF·KYLKENNE

WAXFORD

THE PROVINCE OF MOVNSTER

FIGURE 6.1 Francis Jobson. *The Province of Mounster* (c. 1589). Courtesy of the National Library of Ireland, Shelf Mark 16 B 13.

6
RISE OF THE ENGLISH "NEW MEN": THE MUNSTER PLANTATION

C HANGE WOULD COME RAPIDLY, and with spectacular results, to Ireland's south in the wake of Desmond's failed rebellion. His death and that of many of his followers was a boon for newcomers. His and his confederates' lands—almost half a million acres, some of them among the island's richest farmland—were seized by the crown to be distributed to those in its service. Skilled labor was sorely needed and the population had been devastated. The result was the Munster Plantation, the largest-to-date (if not the first) English colonial scheme in the country. In a colorful map (fig. 6.1), c. 1589, by the surveyor Francis Jobson, English holdings are scattered across the province with green plots labeled according to the new owners.

Plantations were not an exclusively Protestant directive. The first Tudor plantation in Ireland was established at Laois-Offaly (Leix-Offaly) in the midlands during the reign (1552–8) of Queen Mary I, the Catholic half sister of Elizabeth I and wife of Philip II of Spain. Like Laois-Offaly and another, abortive colony in the Ards in Ulster in the early 1570s, the Munster Plantation was based on classical and humanistic principles hearkening back to ancient Rome.

The primary goal was to transform—with order, industry, and innovation—a supposedly "savage," Catholic, backward, and degenerated Irish land into a Protestant and profitable realm that would benefit crown and country. The scheme advocated transplanting subjects of all ranks to rework vast stretches of land recently depopulated by

the wars: what the government termed the "repeopling" of Munster.

With the Munster project, the race was truly on. As in any gold rush, there were winners and losers among both natives and newcomers, and those who could invest the most to begin with were often the most successful. The best-positioned speculators were those with close connections to the London court, men such as Sir Christopher Hatton, the English Lord Chancellor, and the Queen's favorite, Sir Walter Raleigh, who received the largest stake, forty thousand acres, four times the maximum amount stipulated by statute. The Earl of Ormond was the only noble of Irish birth among the original seventeen major grantees (or "undertakers," as they were called) to receive a portion of land.

The project spurred the imagination and tested the expertise of administrators, soldiers, and writers. What reforms were needed? Which ones were possible? What powers should the government have over the undertakers and the many natives who remained? The English Protestant settler Richard Beacon's 1594 policy tract, *Solon His Follie* (see fig. 6.2), is a thinly disguised allegory that answers these questions. Beacon, a planter in County Kerry and Attorney General of Munster, models his conceit on the debates surrounding the ancient Athenian discussions over the colony at Salamis. Strongly influenced by the Italian political theorist Niccolò Machiavelli, he supports colonization, not surprisingly, as well as the use of force under a strong ruler to

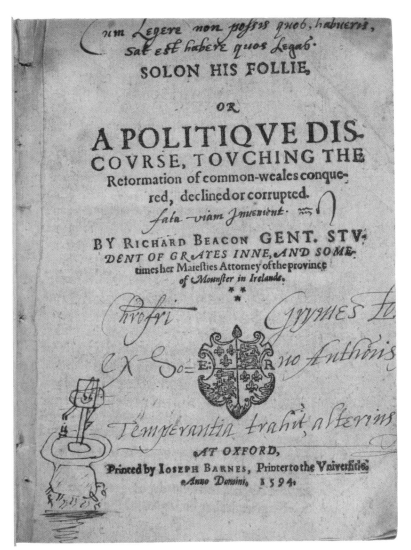

FIGURE 6.2 Richard Beacon. *Solon his follie* (Oxford: Joseph Barnes, 1594), title page. Folger Shelf Mark STC 1653.2.

FIGURE 6.3 William Segar (c. 1554–1633) [attributed]. Portrait of Sir Walter Raleigh (1522–1618), soldier and historian (British, 16th century), oil on canvas. Courtesy of the National Gallery of Ireland.

secure the land and peace. Like others, Beacon believed that a kinder, gentler, civilized society should replace the older, more fractious one after the ground had been broken and well plowed to plant new seeds.

Most famously, the plantation housed Sir Walter Raleigh (fig. 6.3) and the poet he patronized, Edmund Spenser (fig. 6.4),[27] a Londoner who moved to Ireland in 1580 as secretary to Lord Deputy Arthur,

FIGURE 6.4 "Kinnoul Portrait" of Edmund Spenser (c. 1552–99) (England, 16th century), oil on panel. Courtesy of Private Collection/The Bridgeman Art Library.

(*at right*) FIGURE 6.5 Georg Sabinus (1508–60). *Poemata* (Leipzig, 1563?), title page. Folger Shelf Mark V.a.341.

Lord Grey. After 1587, Spenser had his own, independent grant of more than three thousand acres at Kilcolman, County Cork. In many ways, Spenser was typical of the English servitor class, eager to remake himself by using Irish land and wealth to ascend the social hierarchy. He was, however, also atypical: a literary and intellectual giant whose genius flourished far from the metropolis. Once in Munster, Spenser was not isolated in his adopted home; he maintained contact with the literary styles and ideas of England and the wider world. He lived near the administrative seat of the plantation at Mallow (occupied by the provincial president) as well as the walled town of Kilmallock, and

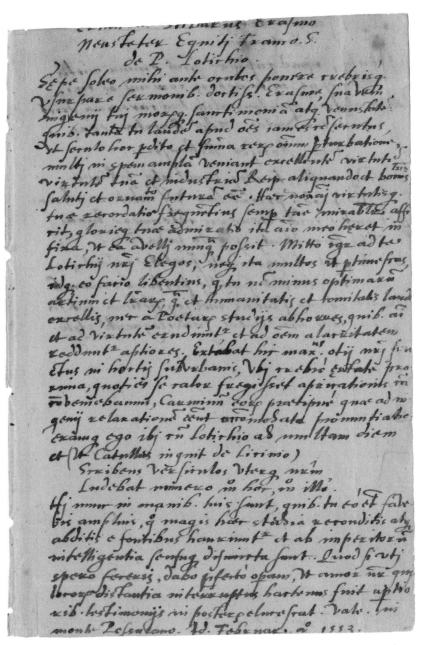

FIGURE 6.6 Edmund Spenser (1552?–99), scribe. Copy of letter from Erhardus Stibarus to Erasmus Neustetter taken from Lotichius, *Elegiarum* (Lyon, 1553), [manuscript] (copied after 1576). Folger Shelf Mark X.d.520.

FIGURE 6.7 Edmund Spenser (1552?–99). *Amoretti and Epithalamion* ([London: P. Short],1595), title page. Folger Shelf Mark STC 23076.

close to the main road between Cork and Limerick, which were important port towns. An extremely rare example of manuscript annotations by him, of uncertain date, demonstrates his continental influences and contacts with German Neo-Latin writing (see figs. 6.5, 6.6).

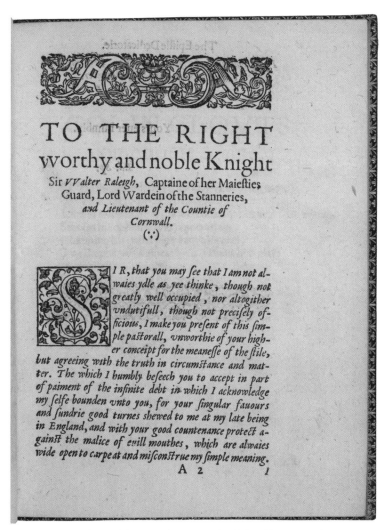

FIGURE 6.8   Edmund Spenser (1552?–99). *Colin Clouts come home againe* (London: Thomas Creede, 1595), sig. A2, Folger Shelf Mark STC 23077 copy 4.

Spenser's own writing includes many genres. Among his poetry, his longest and most famous work is *The Faerie Queene,* an epic romance that both laments and celebrates his precarious position as the Queen's servant in her burgeoning colonial empire. Although not a noble himself,

Spenser wrote about noble characters taken from romance tradition, such as King Arthur, and used their actions to reflect on courtly politics, virtue, religion, and nobility in general. On a more personal level, *Amoretti* – his sonnet sequence – and the celebratory wedding poem *Epithalamion* (fig. 6.7), published together in 1595, chronicle the wooing of his English bride, Elizabeth Boyle, from his tower house in Munster and his marriage to her in a nearby town (probably Youghal). In this collection, Spenser reveals his heart in psychologically penetrating and elegant verse.

His long pastoral poem "Colin Clouts Come Home Againe" (1595; fig. 6.8) is set among his "shepheards nation" (read: planters and locals) in the Munster countryside. It describes identifiable places, such as the ruined monastery of

> Buttevant, [. . .] that auncient Cittie,
> Which Kilnemullah cleped is of old . . .[28]

This apparently innocuous description is a capsule of Spenser's ambition. He would soon own Buttevant, which had been patronized by his noble neighbors, the Old English Barry family. Formerly known by its Gaelic Irish name, Kilnemullah, Buttevant had been founded as a friary and renamed by the Barrys according to their family motto, *Boutez en avant* (roughly: "Charge ahead"). Now it was Spenser's turn to charge ahead: His travel to and "travail" in Ireland set him on a path toward enrichment and greater social standing amid the destruction of the old order—very good progress for a scholarship boy from London.

Among Spenser's friends in Ireland was his fellow writer and colonial Lodowick Bryskett, an Anglo-Italian who translated the humanist dialogue by the Italian author Cinthio into *A Discourse of Civill Life* (see page 16). Bryskett also wrote poetry, including an elegy to the departed spirit of Sir Philip Sidney (a.k.a. "Phillisides"), which influenced Milton's *Lycidas* and appears in the volume *Colin Clouts Come Home Againe* (see fig. 6.9):

49

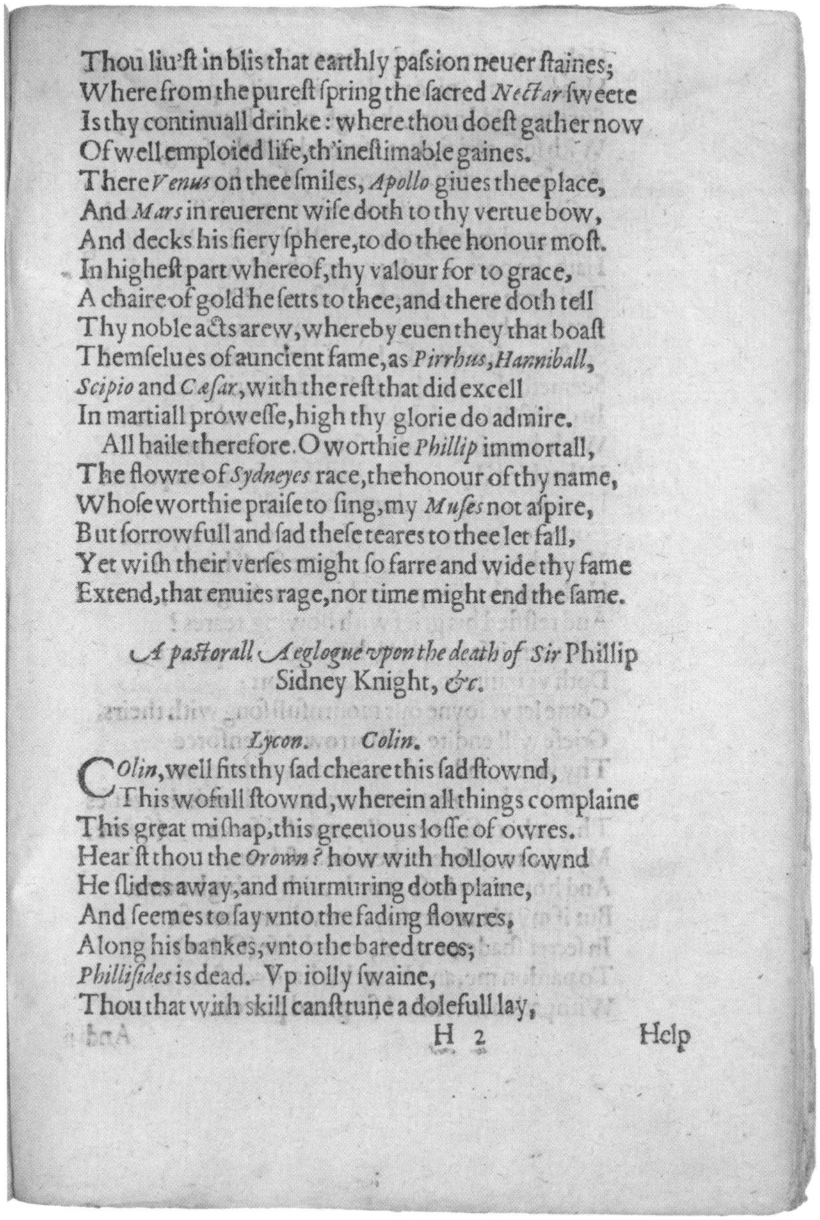

Thou liu'st in blis that earthly pasion neuer staines;
Where from the purest spring the sacred *Nectar* sweete
Is thy continuall drinke: where thou doest gather now
Of well emploied life, th'inestimable gaines.
There *Venus* on thee smiles, *Apollo* giues thee place,
And *Mars* in reuerent wise doth to thy vertue bow,
And decks his fiery sphere, to do thee honour most.
In highest part whereof, thy valour for to grace,
A chaire of gold he setts to thee, and there doth tell
Thy noble acts arew, whereby euen they that boast
Themselues of auncient fame, as *Pirrhus*, *Hanniball*,
Scipio and *Cæsar*, with the rest that did excell
In martiall prowesse, high thy glorie do admire.
    All haile therefore. O worthie *Phillip* immortall,
The flowre of *Sydneyes* race, the honour of thy name,
Whose worthie praise to sing, my *Muses* not aspire,
But sorrowfull and sad these teares to thee let fall,
Yet with their verses might so farre and wide thy fame
Extend, that enuies rage, nor time might end the same.

A pastorall Aeglogue vpon the death of Sir Phillip
Sidney Knight, *&c.*

Lycon.   *Colin.*

C*olin*, well fits thy sad cheare this sad stownd,
   This wofull stownd, wherein all things complaine
This great mishap, this greeuous losse of owres.
Hear'st thou the *Orown*? how with hollow sownd
He slides away, and murmuring doth plaine,
And seemes to say vnto the fading flowres,
Along his bankes, vnto the bared trees;
Phillisides is dead. Vp iolly swaine,
Thou that with skill canst tune a dolefull lay,

     A   H 2   Help

FIGURE 6.9 Lodowick Bryskett. "A pastorall Aeglogue upon the death of
Sir Phillip Sidney Knight, &c." in Edmund Spenser (1552?–99).
Colin Clouts come home again (London: Thomas Creede, 1595), sig. H2.
Folger Shelf Mark STC 23077 copy 2.

Colin, well fits thy sad cheare this sad stownd,
This wofull stownd, wherein all things complaine
This great mishap, this greevous losse of owres.
Hear'st thou the *Orown*? how with hollow sownd
He slides away, and murmuring doth plaine,
And seemes to say unto the fading flowres,
Along his bankes, unto the bared trees;
Phillisides is dead. Up jolly swaine,
Thou that with skill canst tune a dolefull lay,
Help him to mourn.[29]

Bryskett, alias Lycon, laments with Spenser, alias Colin, over a weeping Irish stream, the Orown.[30] Both poets felt keenly the loss of one of England's guiding military and poetic lights, the Protestant Sir Philip, killed in 1586 while fighting the Spanish in the Netherlands. Philip, the son of the Lord Deputy of Ireland, Sir Henry (see page 14), had visited Ireland in the mid-1570s. As far as Spenser and Bryskett were concerned, in their writing all Ireland and England would mourn Philip's loss.

The end of Spenser's Munster dreams came swiftly and through war, as the Ulster nobles O'Neill, O'Donnell, and Maguire swept south to clear the land of such colonial upstarts. An Irish poem by Eochaidh Ó hEodhusa (O'Hussey; fig. 6.10) celebrates the Munster campaign of his patron, Hugh Maguire, a bright flame in the depth of a Gaelic winter that destroys the white-coated houses of the southern colony.

Nárab aithreach leis ná leam
a thursu timcheall Éireann;
go ndeach tharaim — ná tí m'ol —
an ní fá ngabhaim gúasacht.

Gidh eadh, is adhbhar téighthe
dhá ghnúis shúaithnigh shoiléirthe
slios gach múir ghormsháothraigh gil
'na dhlúimh thonngháothmhair theintigh.[31]

I hope neither he nor I
will regret this circuit of Ireland
I sense danger in it:
may it pass — let my fear not come
and what ever the possible losses,

And yet — there is something to warm
his honest and noble face:
all the castle walls blue-burning
in a pall of wind-tossed fire![32]

Maguire had believed that his own lands in Fermanagh, in the north, were slated for plantation; in 1594, this helped to push him into rebellion, and O'Neill soon followed. Maguire had no love for the planters, and in the wake of that winter campaign, Spenser was burned out of his castle in Kilcolman — this prophetically named "Hap-Hazard" — and died penniless in London, the city of his youth.

Sir Walter Raleigh soon thereafter sold his Munster lands at a very low price to another New English upstart, Richard Boyle. The circle had closed on the first generation of the Munster Plantation.

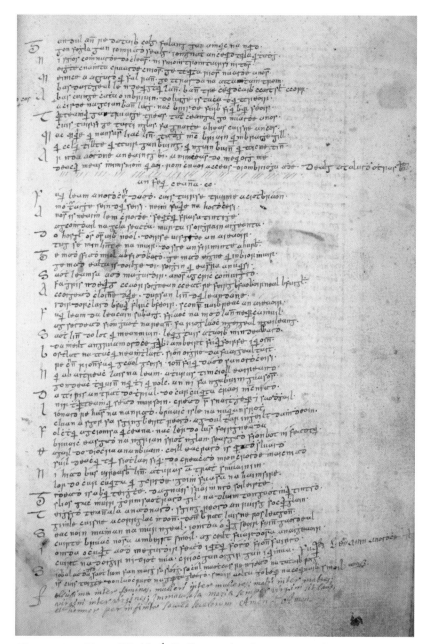

FIGURE 6.10 Feargal Dubh Ó Gadhra, scribe. Court Verse. O'Gara manuscript (17th century), 5: Hugh Maguire poem. Courtesy of the Royal Irish Academy, Shelf Mark MS 23 F 16.

51

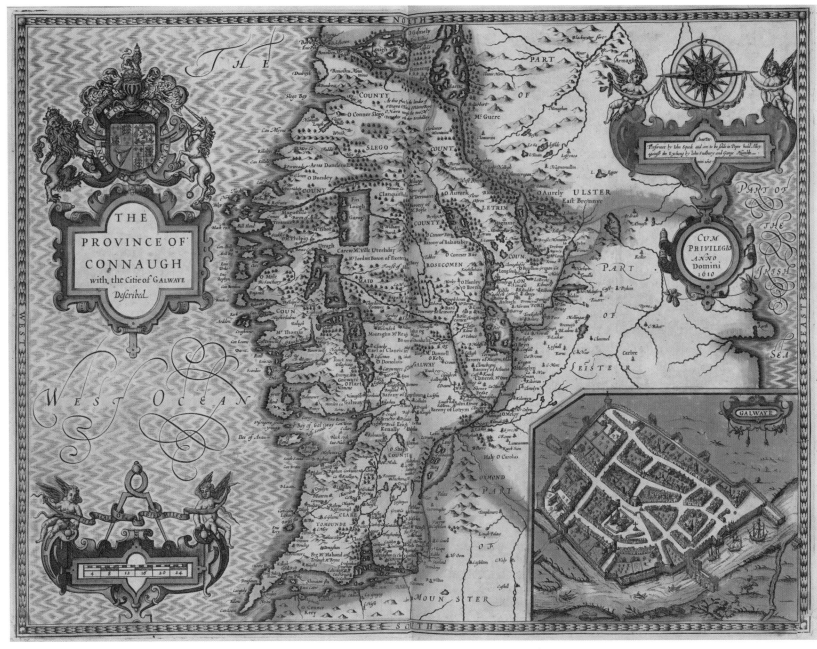

FIGURE 7.1 John Speed (1552?–1629). *Theatre of the Empire of Great Britaine*
(London: [Thomas Snodham], 1616), plate after page 143: Province of Connaugh. Folger Shelf Mark STC 23044.

7
BREAKING THE WEST:
QUEENS, CAPTAINS, AND NOBILITY IN CONNACHT

[T]he husbandman must first break the land, before it be made capable of good seed: and when it is thoroughly broken and manured, if he do not forthwith cast good seed into it, it will grow wild again, and bear nothing but weeds. So a barbarous country must be first broken by a war, before it will be capable of good government . . .³³ — JOHN DAVIES

THE PROVINCE OF CONNACHT, in Ireland's west, experienced the heady mix of negotiation and resistance, alliance and violence, that marked earlier English–Irish contact in Leinster and Munster. Yet the government of Connacht was particularly prone to abuse by nominally loyal officials operating largely outside of crown control in a remote part of the realm (fig. 7.1).

Like viceroys before him, Lord Deputy William Fitzwilliam (see fig. 7.2) was charged with bringing recalcitrant Gaels and Old English under crown authority. He had another headache, however: New English administrators who took the law into their own hands

and antagonized the local population. "Captains" such as Richard Bingham (see fig. 7.3), "the flail of Connacht" and later president of the province, were instrumental in inciting rebellion among the locals. The inability of Fitzwilliam to curb them alienated both native Irish and Old English from the crown.

Not all entrenched interests in the west suffered in the late-Tudor and early-Stuart periods. The O'Briens, a native Irish kingship of ancient ancestry (the famous high king of Ireland Brian Boru [d. 1014] was an O'Brien), continued to rule as earls of Thomond and flourished during these turbulent times. They did so in part because of their unswerving loyalty to the crown in war, their Protestantism, and also the fatal missteps of their rivals.

The deeply complex nature of nobility in this period is dramatically captured by Dohmnaill Mac Bruaideadha, the latest in a long and distinguished line of *ollúna filíochta* (chief poets) to the O'Briens. The occasion for the following verse was the coming to power of Connor O'Brien as chief of the name and third Earl of Thomond. A fundamental component of Mac Bruaideadha's post was the penning of

FIGURE 7.2 English School. Portrait of Sir William Fitzwilliam (1529–99), Lord Deputy of Ireland, 1595. Courtesy of a private collection.

54

FIGURE 7.3 Unknown artist. *Sir Richard Bingham* (1528–99), oil on panel, 1564. Courtesy of the National Portrait Gallery, London.

poems for just such events. The resulting work, however, is a curious one, for this eulogistic tradition was directed at the Gaelic *ríthe* (kings), not English-style earls. And yet the occasion celebrated O'Brien's English title as well, and the poet returns to the ancient motif of Irish noble as regional king (of "Tuadhmhumha," that is Thomond, or North Munster), at the same time demonstrating a new flexibility in poetic subject (fig. 7.4):

An d'iarraidh creach nó cána,
nó créad as cúis tionóla
fa Chliagh ródghloin na sriobh seang
a-niogh ag ógbhoidh Éireann?

Dá ríoghadh i ráith Luimnigh
ós chionn an cláir Thuadhmhuimhnigh
d'fhuil na mBrian gidh bé dhleaghar
is é as ciall don chruinneaghadh.[34]

Is it plunder of cess?
what causes the gathering
of all Éire's soldiers around
fair-roaded calm-streamed Cliu?

The appointing at Luimneach's fort [i.e., Limerick]
of the rightful one of the race
of Brian as King over the plain of Tuadhmhumha—
that is the meaning of the gathering.[35]

Was this an inauguration poem for a king or for an earl? Whatever it was in the mind of the poet, it is apparent that this is a transitional work, one that offers a snapshot of changing notions of nobility in this colonial setting.

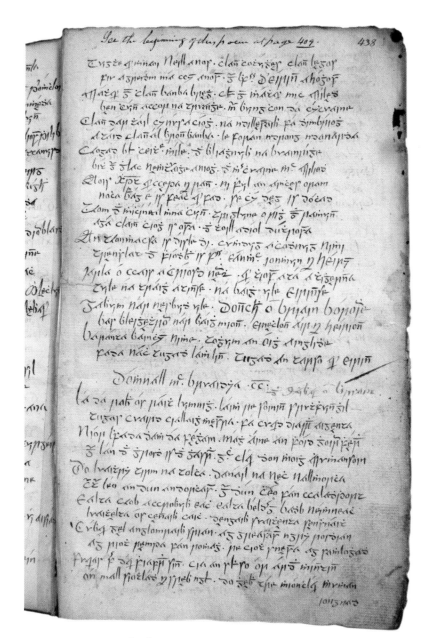

FIGURE 7.4 Mícheál Óg Ó Longáin (1766–1837), scribe. A collection of scraps of manuscripts written at various times and in various places [manuscript], 1795–1821, 1833, page 438: inauguration poem to the Earl of Thomond. Courtesy of the Royal Irish Academy, Shelf Mark MS 23 G 24.

55

(*left*) FIGURE 7.5
Sir Anthony van Dyck
(1599–1641).
The Marchioness of Worcester
(c. 1637). Courtesy of the
Baltimore Museum of Art.

(*right*) FIGURE 7.6
The Pirate Queen
([New York]: Playbill,
[2007]), cover.

(*facing page*) FIGURE 7.7
Rockfleet Castle on Clew
Bay, County Mayo, Ireland
(Pirate Queen Tower
House). Photo courtesy
of the Irish Image
Collection/Getty Images.

A more clear-cut anglicization of a noble O'Brien can be seen in a portrait of Margaret O'Brien, daughter of Donough, the fourth Earl of Thomond (fig. 7.5). It shows this scion of Irish kings resplendent in the aristocratic fashions of mid-seventeenth-century Britain. The artist, van Dyck, shares none of the confusion experienced by the poet Mac Bruaideadha regarding the basis of his subject's nobility.

Curiously, the region's best-known noble figure today—Grace O'Malley, the "Pirate Queen" of Clew Bay, County Mayo—was a relatively obscure figure in her own day. A musical based on her life debuted in 2006 but quickly sank on Broadway: evidence of history's continued, if not universal, fascination with her and her story (figs. 7.6, 7.7). O'Malley was a member of a minor noble family in Mayo and a unique example of an Irish female ruler. On the death of her husband, one of the powerful O'Flahertys, she proved an able sea captain and

negotiator who did business up and down the west coast. She took a second husband, Richard "an Iarainn" ("Iron Richard"), of the Old English Clanwilliam Burkes of Mayo, and their son Theobald became Viscount Mayo in 1627. She met Sir Philip Sidney during his visit to Ireland in 1576 and was long rumored, if without truth, to have met Queen Elizabeth in London in 1593 (see fig. 7.8). O'Malley nevertheless demonstrates that female rulers, although rare, could flourish in both of the Tudor realms.

As in Munster, Connacht attracted its share of New English writers. Barnabe Googe (1540–94), for example, was a noted mid-Tudor author of antipapal polemics, philosophy about the soul, satirical allegories, poetry, and other writings. A jack-of-all-trades, in 1574 he served as emissary to the first Earl of Essex in Ulster on behalf of Lord Burghley and from 1582 to 1585 as Provost of Connacht. To Googe,

Ireland was a "purgatory" that helped to secure his more blissful retirement in Alvingham, England. After visiting Ulster (where he would have become acquainted with the colonial project in the Ards) and before his service in Connacht, Googe translated the German writer Conrad Heresbach's popular manual of husbandry, published as *The Whole Art and Trade of Husbandry* (London 1578; see fig. 7.9). It opens with an elaborate dedication to Lord Deputy Fitzwilliam: One implication is that an agricultural reform treatise published in England might easily benefit Ireland as well.[36]

The descendants of Connacht's planters would in turn become the inspiration of great literature. Sir John King (d. 1637) flourished in Connacht after arriving in Ireland in 1585 as secretary to Richard Bingham, a post similar to the one Spenser held under Lord Grey. Sir John became a member of the Irish Privy Council and earned a

58

FIGURE 7.8 Artist unknown, attributed to the school of Marcus Gheeraerts the Younger (c. 1561/62–1636). Portrait of Elizabeth I (1533–1603), oil on oak panels, c. 1593. Courtesy of the Elizabethan Gardens, Manteo, North Carolina.

FIGURE 7.9 Conrad Heresbach (1496–1576). *Foure bookes of husbandry* (London: [John Kingston], 1578), (ij)r. Folger Shelf Mark STC 13197 copy 2.

knighthood for his service. He amassed large amounts of property, mainly in and around Boyle, County Roscommon, under dubious circumstances, and spent much of his time in Dublin working the corridors of power (he had a house there as well). His son Edward (1611/12–37), a Protestant minister who drowned crossing the Irish Sea, is mourned by his classmate John Milton as "Lycidas" in the poem by that name (1638; fig. 7.10). The poem belongs to a collection of

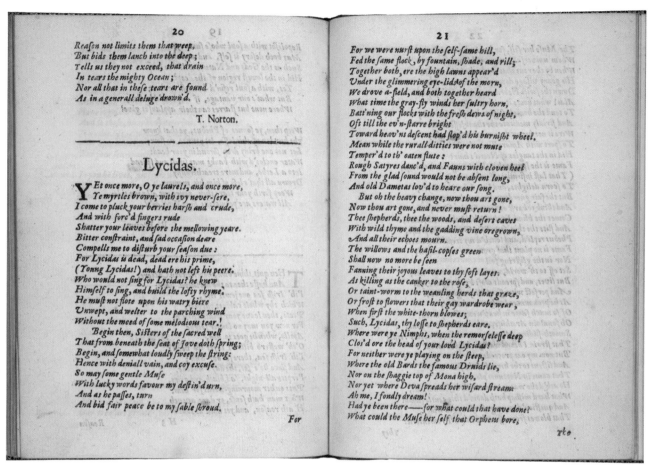

FIGURE 7.10 John Milton (1608–74). "Lycidas" from *Justa Edouardo King naufrago*
(Cambridge: Thomas Buck, 1638), last section, 20–21. Folger Shelf Mark STC 14964.

59

elegies composed in England for Edward soon after his death. Edward was sailing home to Ireland when he famously drowned on that "perfidious bark," and Milton looked westward for models of grief: The poem is strongly influenced by both Spenser's "Colin Clouts Come Home Againe" and the elegies for Sir Philip Sidney, set in Ireland, by Spenser and Bryskett (see page 50) in the same volume (1595).

Sir John King's second son would prosper in Ireland. Sir Robert

King (d. 1657) was a prominent Cromwellian during the Civil Wars and his son John (c. 1620–76) became first Baron Kingston at the Restoration (1660). Sir Richard Bingham's descendants also flourished, becoming Lords Lucan, a lordship close to Dublin. Within a few generations, power ill gained in the broken west would be translated into respectability and nobility in the eastern establishment.

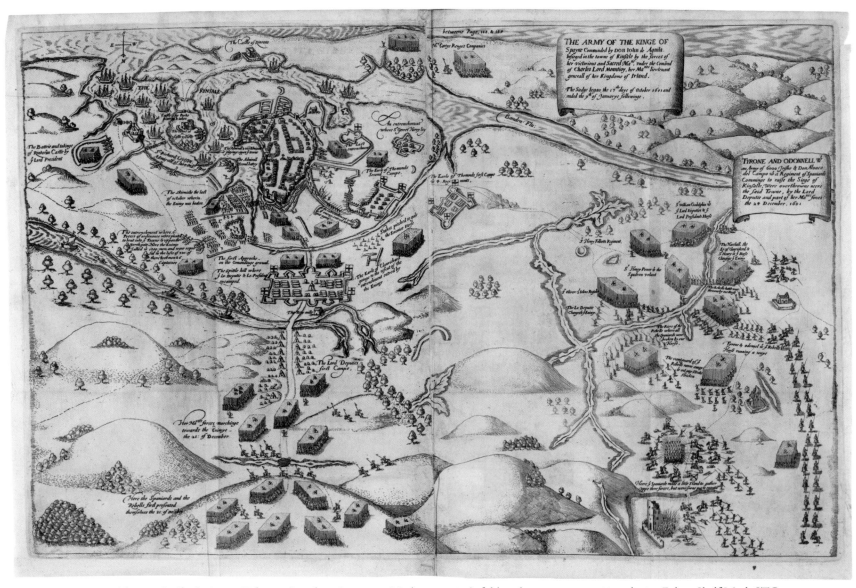

FIGURE 8.1 Sir Thomas Stafford. *Pacata Hibernia* (London: Augustine Mathewes, 1633), foldout between pages 188 and 189. Folger Shelf Mark STC 23132a.

8

THE NINE YEARS' WAR

THE NINE YEARS' WAR (1594–1603) was a watershed conflict in Irish history, typically taken to mark the end of the Gaelic order. It was also a major event in England, as it cost more than all of Queen Elizabeth's other military forays combined. Among its victims was the dashing second Earl of Essex, the Queen's final favorite, and it concluded only a few days after her own death in London. This protracted rebellion against English rule in Ireland began in Ulster; had its climax at the Battle of Kinsale (1601), at the opposite end of the country; and reached its denouement back in Ulster. A major consequence was the destruction of the Munster Plantation in the south and, after many punishments, pardons, and minor rebellions, the beginning of the Ulster Plantation in the north (see page 81).

What began as tussles between nobility and the crown in the north eventually grew into a major international and religious conflict. Having witnessed the fate of Desmond, whose patrimony became the Munster Plantation, the great northern lords Hugh O'Neill, Earl of Tyrone, and Red Hugh O'Donnell, Lord of Tyrconnell, conspired to resist crown incursions on their local authority. In 1594, proxy battles and diplomatic brinkmanship finally gave way to armed conflict.

Commanding the "rebels" was the wily and supremely capable Hugh O'Neill, an innovative strategist and Catholic who was as comfortable at an English dinner table as at an Irish one. He sought and received help from such local magnates as Red Hugh O'Donnell, as

well as from King Philip II of Spain and the pope. His enemies were crown forces, by no means exclusively English soldiers and commanders but rather of mixed ethnicity, including, as leaders, the Old English earls of Ormond (a Protestant) and Clanricard (a Catholic) and the Gaelic Irish Earl of Thomond (a Protestant). They served under the overall command of the English, including the second Earl of Essex, who launched a meandering and abortive campaign (1599–1600) with the largest expeditionary force ever to be sent to Ireland.

Essex's successor as commander of crown forces in Ireland, Robert Blount, Lord Mountjoy, proved far more successful. His finest hour came at Kinsale, County Cork, in 1601, when his army simultaneously defeated Spanish and Irish occupying forces near the town. A large foldout map in Thomas Stafford's *Pacata Hibernia* ("The Pacification of Ireland," London 1633; fig. 8.1) shows the ensuing battle: Mountjoy's army was caught between a Spanish expeditionary force in the town, which Mountjoy had besieged, and Tyrone's and O'Donnell's combined army approaching from the north, which had encircled them. Mountjoy met his opponents in a set-piece counterattack and routed them.

A "scorched-earth campaign" mopped up the country afterward, further crippling the native powers and driving into exile many Irishmen from all over the country. These included the Munster Lord Donal Cam O'Sullivan Beare, first Count of Berehaven, an early

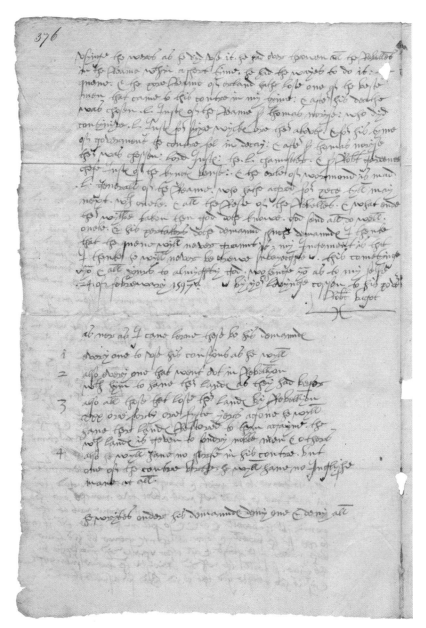

62

FIGURE 8.2 Letter from Robert Bagot, Dublin to Richard Bagot, Blithfield [manuscript], (February 24, 1598), fol. 1v. Folger Shelf Mark L.a.85.

example of what would prove a long line of Irish nobles (and commoners) who made names for themselves in the competing empire of Catholic Spain.

Events would force significant realignments of Irish nobility, mostly to their detriment. O'Donnell would leave for Spain after Kinsale in the hope of securing additional support for his campaign, only to die from illness. O'Neill, a bloodied and tired badger backed into his northern den, was pardoned and retained his title, but was subjected to intense pressure by the administration and later fled to the Continent in the vain hope of renewed support.

Even in the private papers of the English Bagot family (one of whom served in Ireland at the time) are found Hugh O'Neill's demands to the crown. The following excerpt speaks directly to resentment over the transfer of lands from ancient nobles to new (fig. 8.2):

also all those that loste the[i]r land[es] by Rebellion xxx [30] ore forty ore fyfte yers agone he wyll haue th[er] land[es] Restored to them agane. the w[hi]ch land[es] is geven to sondry noble men & others.[37]

Red Hugh's control of the O'Donnell lordship passed to his brother Rory, who took an English-style noble title, Earl of Tyrconnell, as part of his promise of fealty. He was the first of the dynasty to take one: Rather than an indication of social elevation, it was a sign of obedience. Despite this, he too ended his days in continental exile. Not all Irish nobles were lost or displaced, however: The loyal servants Ormond, Clanricard, and Thomond boosted themselves in British society thanks to their work for the winning side.

An English manuscript miscellany contains documents pertaining to the second Earl of Essex and his campaign in Ireland. It includes policy tracts like Spenser's prose dialogue *A View of the Present State of Ireland* (c. 1596; published 1633; fig. 8.3). Spenser influenced writers, administrators, and commanders with his advice on Irish customs,

FIGURE 8.3 Edmund Spenser (1552?–99). *A view of the present state of Ireland.* In a miscellany on religion and state affairs, 1559–1601 [manuscript] (compiled c. 1601), 137. Folger Shelf Mark V.b.214.

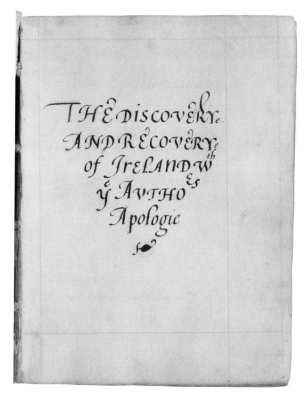

FIGURE 8.4 Thomas Lee (1551/2–1601). "The discoverye and recoverye of Ireland" [manuscript] (c. 1600), title page. Folger Shelf Mark V.a.475.

63

genealogies, forts, and garrisons, along with a strident call to arms on behalf of the New English. It is thought that Spenser had in mind the second Earl of Essex in his rousing call for a chief governor to take absolute control of the country.

Another writer featured in the same manuscript miscellany is the ambitious, brave, and well-connected Captain Thomas Lee, an Englishman who wrote many tracts of advice, among them "The Discoverye and Recoverye of Ireland with the Author's Apologie" (c. 1600; fig. 8.4). In it he invokes the specter of an enhanced Irish nobility, should the house of Desmond return in conjunction with the house of O'Neill. As Captain Lee warns, the "arch traytor" O'Neill, Earl of

Tyrone, has taken upon himself the Queen's power of aristocratic creation and has "made" the "new earle of desmond." This refers to O'Neill's illicit granting in February 1600 of the title Earl of Desmond to James Fitzthomas Fitzgerald, the so-called Súgán or "Straw Rope" earl, illegitimate half brother of the "Rebel" fifteenth Earl of Desmond. O'Neill, rebelling against the English crown, was simultaneously granting English-style titles as a method of consolidating his power.

Lee, like O'Neill, was a highly mercurial figure: He had been a friend and confidant of the Earl of Tyrone before the Nine Years' War, for example, and married two Catholic Old Englishwomen (in 1579 and 1595). He was well connected at court (a cousin of Sir Henry Lee, the Queen's champion) and posed for one of the most iconic and bizarre images involving Ireland in the period, his full-length portrait in half-English, half-Irish fashion by Marcus Gheeraerts the Younger (fig. 8.5). Lee's flowery, open shirt, bare legs, supple "dart" (an Irish throwing spear), and pistol at the ready make him a perfect pinup for the preening masculine characters who used the battlefield to advance a bold image of themselves at court. The proud and foolish Lee met his end in 1601, with the Earl of Essex, during Essex's rebellion in London.

Other publications demonstrate the excitement and interest in England and elsewhere caused by the war. For example, *A Letter from a Souldier of Good Place in Ireland, to his Friend in London, Touching the Notable Victorie of her Maiesties Forces there, against the Spaniards, and Irish Rebels: And of the Yeelding up of Kynsale, and other Places there Held by the Spanyards* (London 1602; fig. 8.6), by "I.E.," reports on the war and celebrates the fall of the old nobility and the rise of the new from the point of view of a common soldier. Its cheap production standard means that it probably reached a wide audience. Thomas

FIGURE 8.5 Marcus Gheeraerts the Younger (1561/2–1636). Portrait of Captain Thomas Lee (1594), oil on canvas. Courtesy of Tate Britain.

Stafford's grand narrative of events, *Pacata Hibernia* (London 1633), maps and describes much of the war and praises the role of New Englishman Sir George Carew, Lord President of Munster and later Earl of Totnes, in particular in his efforts to pacify Munster.

Drama of the period also took note of Ireland's agony and that of the earls of Tyrone and Essex. Heywood's *The Famous Historye of the Life and Death of Captaine Thomas Stukeley* (c. 1596; published 1605; see page 20) treats events from the 1560s involving a different "Oneill"—that is, the powerful Shane, then chief of the dynasty and scourge of Sir Henry Sidney's deputyship. It was written and produced in London against the backdrop of the Nine Years' War; thus reference to one O'Neill evokes the specter of another.

Henry V (c. 1599; see fig. 8.7), Shakespeare's patriotic war play par excellence, celebrates King Henry's stunning fifteenth-century victory in the hostile terrain at Agincourt, France: an action clearly analogous to a hoped-for conclusion to the Tudor conquest of Ireland. The prologue to Act 5 (not published until the First Folio, in 1623) imagines Henry returning to London after Agincourt as the savior of the realm:

> . . . But now behold,
> In the quick forge and working-house of thought,
> How London doth pour out her citizens.
> The Mayor and all his brethren, in best sort,
> Like to the senators of th'antique Rome
> With the plebeians swarming at their heels,
> Go forth and fetch their conqu'ring Caesar in—
> As, by a lower but high-loving likelihood,
> Were now the General of our gracious Empress—
> As in good time he may—from Ireland coming,
> Bringing rebellion broached on his sword,
> How many would the peaceful city quit
> To welcome him![38]

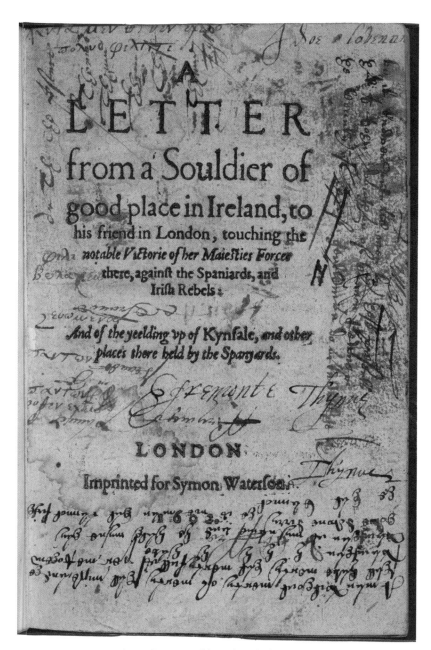

FIGURE 8.6 *A letter from a Souldier of good place in Ireland* (London: [Thomas Creede?], 1602), title page. Folger Shelf Mark STC 7434 copy 1.

66

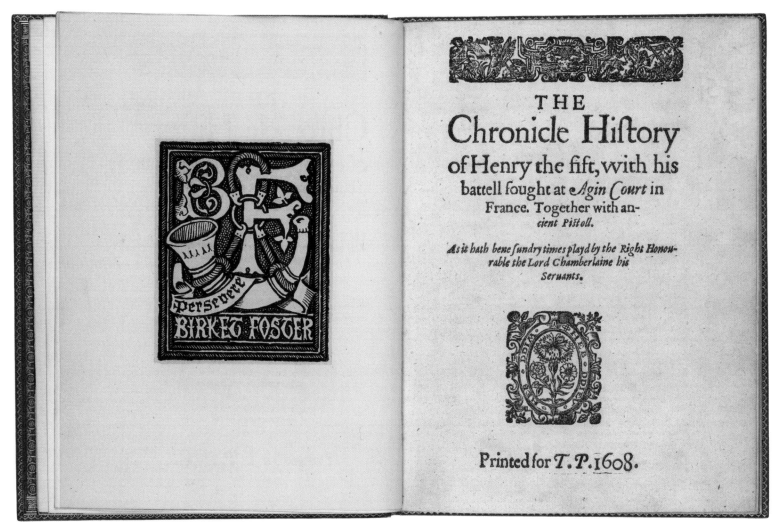

FIGURE 8.7 William Shakespeare (1564–1616). *Henry V* ([London]: Printed for T.P., 1608), title page. Folger Shelf Mark STC 22291 copy 1.

Most critics understand "the General" as referring to Essex, although it could refer to Mountjoy. Intriguingly, another Henry—that is, Wriothesley, the third Earl of Southampton (fig. 8.8), Shakespeare's former patron—served Essex in Ireland as General of the Horse (a title held also by Bertram in *All's Well That Ends Well,* written c. 1602). After their joint return from Ireland, Southampton backed Essex's disastrous coup attempt against Elizabeth in 1601. Ironically, Ireland did nothing but increase Essex's isolation from the court and contributed to his eventual downfall and death; he himself played the rebel then.

67

FIGURE 8.8
Daniel Mytens (1590–1648)
[after]. Portrait of Henry Wriothesley,
Earl of Southampton (not before 1620).
Folger Shelf Mark FPb55.

Henry V was performed in London around the time the earls were mustering their troops for the Irish campaign. It features Captain Mac-Morris, an Irish character with an Old English name fighting for the English. He wonders "what ish my nation?" and threatens to cut off the head of anyone who insults him or it. England's martial "band of brothers," celebrated so famously in King Henry's "St. Crispin's Day" speech in act IV, thereby consists of warriors from many nations: a forerunner of British pluralities to come.

FIGURES 9.1 AND 9.2
John Speed (1552?–1629).
Theatre of the Empire of Great Britaine (London: [Thomas Snodham], 1616), Folger Shelf Mark STC 23044.
(*left*) frontispiece
(*right*) detail from plate between pages 137 and 138.

9
JAMES VI AND I AND THE THREE KINGDOMS, 1603-25

WHEN HUGH O'NEILL finally surrendered to Lord Deputy Mountjoy, in March 1603, Queen Elizabeth I had, unbeknownst to O'Neill, recently died; the old Irish nobility had been negotiating with ghosts. A new Stuart administration centered in London under the new king, James I (James VI of Scotland), replaced the Tudors and heralded a gaudy spring of peace. James quickly began revamping the nobility of his realms.

James, who claimed Irish descent through the legendary king Fergus, created Great Britain and gained political capital by becoming King of Ireland as well as of England and Scotland (fig. 9.1). To judge from the illustrations in John Speed's *Theatre of the Empire of Great Britaine* (1616; fig. 9.2; see also fig. 2.1), dedicated to the King, all citizens were made aware of the King's power to rule and unite his various realms. The detail in figure 9.2, which comes from the margins of the map of Ireland, indicates a lively ethnographic interest in the various social classes then to be found on the island: "gentle," "civil," and "wild." A later historical-topographical work excerpted from various authors, *Respublica, sive Status regni Scotiae et Hiberniae* (Leiden 1627), demonstrates the uncomfortable working relationship between the two kingdoms: A civilized-looking Scotsman stands, hand on sword, across from a mantle-clad Irishman holding a harp. The Irishman's retainer, with spear, is behind him. The harp, front and center, promotes harmony between them but the weapons remain at the ready (see fig. 9.3).

Despite the defeat of the Gaelic old order in the Nine Years' War, bardic intellectuals welcomed the new king with traditional tributes that praised him as the natural spouse of Ireland. The classic example is the Donegal poet Fearghal Óg Mac an Bhaird's "Trí coróna i gcairt Sheamais" (Three Crowns in James's Charter; see fig. 9.4). The Mac an Bhaird family were traditional *ollúna* to the O'Donnells, but here the court poet aims his encomiastic talents at a new master:

> *Fada a-tá i dtairngire dhuit*
> *críoch Sagsan—is iul orrdhruic;*
> *duit is dú Éire amhlaidh;*
> *is tú a céile ar chomhardhaibh.*[39]

> The Saxon's land has been long—
> 'tis well known—prophesied for thee;
> so too is Éire due to thee;
> thou art her spouse by all signs.[40]

Displayed here, too, is a work from c. 1603 detailing the feats of Ossian, hero of ancient Irish myth (see fig. 9.5). Never mind the new dispensation: Irish scribes continued to copy out the great native myth cycles with their appeal to nobility and commoner alike.

The Irish language was increasingly entering the world of print, at times in the interest of the new king's efforts at ensuring religious uniformity across the realms. William Daniel, Protestant Archbishop

70

FIGURE 9.3 *Respublica sive status regni Scotiae et Hiberniae*
([Leiden]: Ex officina Elzeviriana, 1627), title page.
Folger Shelf Mark 160- 780q.

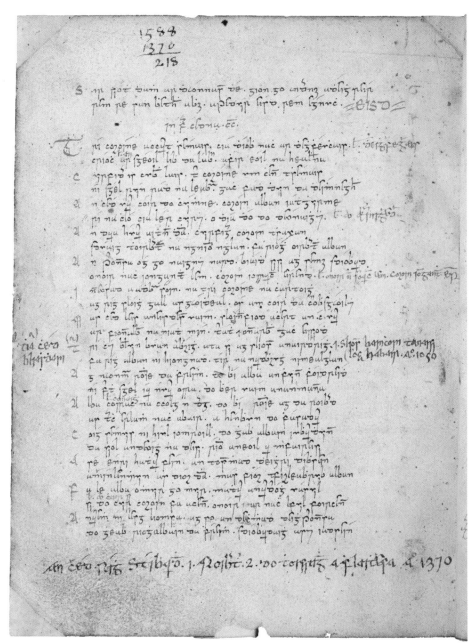

FIGURE 9.4 Poem in praise of James I, from *The book of the O'Conor Don*
[manuscript], fol. 406v. Courtesy of Clonalis House.

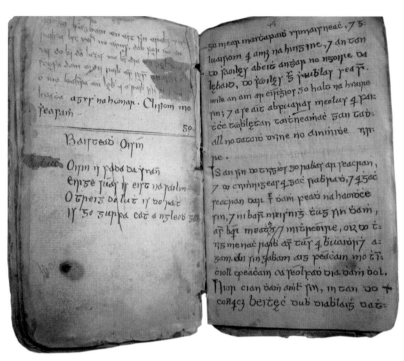

FIGURE 9.5 Transcribed by Domhnall ac Mothánna/Domhnal ac Taig. [Tales, Ossianic verse], [manuscript] (c. 1603?). Courtesy of the University of Wisconsin, Madison.

FIGURE 9.6 Church of England. *Leabhar na nUrnaightheadh gComhchoidchiond* (Dublin: Sheon Francke, 1608), title page. Courtesy of The Pierpont Morgan Library, New York, Shelf Mark PML 27709. Photo by Graham Haber.

of Tuam (Galway), translated the official church's *Book of Common Prayer,* published in 1608 as the *Leabhar na nUrnaightheadh gComhchoidchiond* (fig. 9.6). This was no simple literal translation of an English model; it was a theologically rigorous production that benefited from Daniel's access to the then in-progress King James Bible, and it was written so as to reflect the author's own preferences for local practice and was rendered in effective Irish idiom. Elegantly presented in the contemporary fashion for black and red ink, the book is a landmark in the development of Irish print and linguistics. It was not, however, an evangelizing success, and disappointment over the persistence of Catholicism in the island would drive Daniel to drink and an early death.

English poets, too, welcomed James's rule over the Gaels. Ben Jonson's *Irish Masque at Court* (1613; published 1640), in fact, seems to mimic Mac an Bhaird's panegyric. An Irish "bard," singing in English, celebrates James as the sun king and husband of the realm who heralds a new spring for Britain (see fig. 9.7). His warm light enables the Irish to "slough" off their mantles like so many emerging butterflies should they obey him:

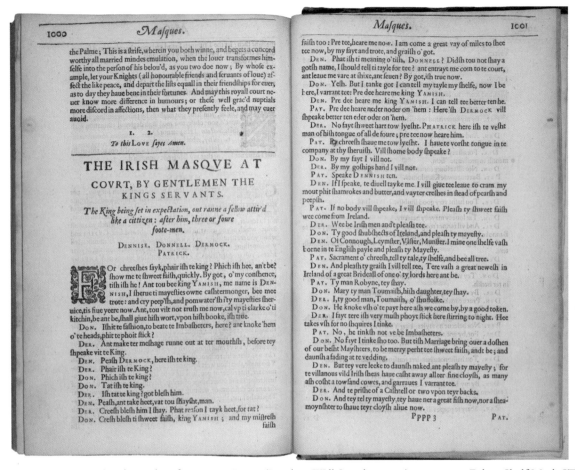

FIGURE 9.7 Ben Jonson (1573?–1637). *The workes of Benjamin Jonson* (London: Will Stansby, 1616), 1000–01. Folger Shelf Mark STC 14751 copy 5.

Bow both your heads at once and hearts;
Obedience doth not well in parts.
It is but standing in his eye,
You'll feel yourselves changed, by and by.
Few live that know how quick a spring
Works in the presence of a king.
'Tis done by this, your slough let fall,
And come forth new-born creatures all.[41]

The entertainment's performance in London, before the King and his court, stereotyped the Irish as subservient buffoons badly in need of the good government that James will offer. The performance was timed to coincide with an embassy of Old English Dubliners, whose complaints about misgovernment fell on deaf ears. Serious tensions between the Old English of the Pale and the English court in London continued to simmer, and the comical and patronizing "stage Irishman" took further shape.

72

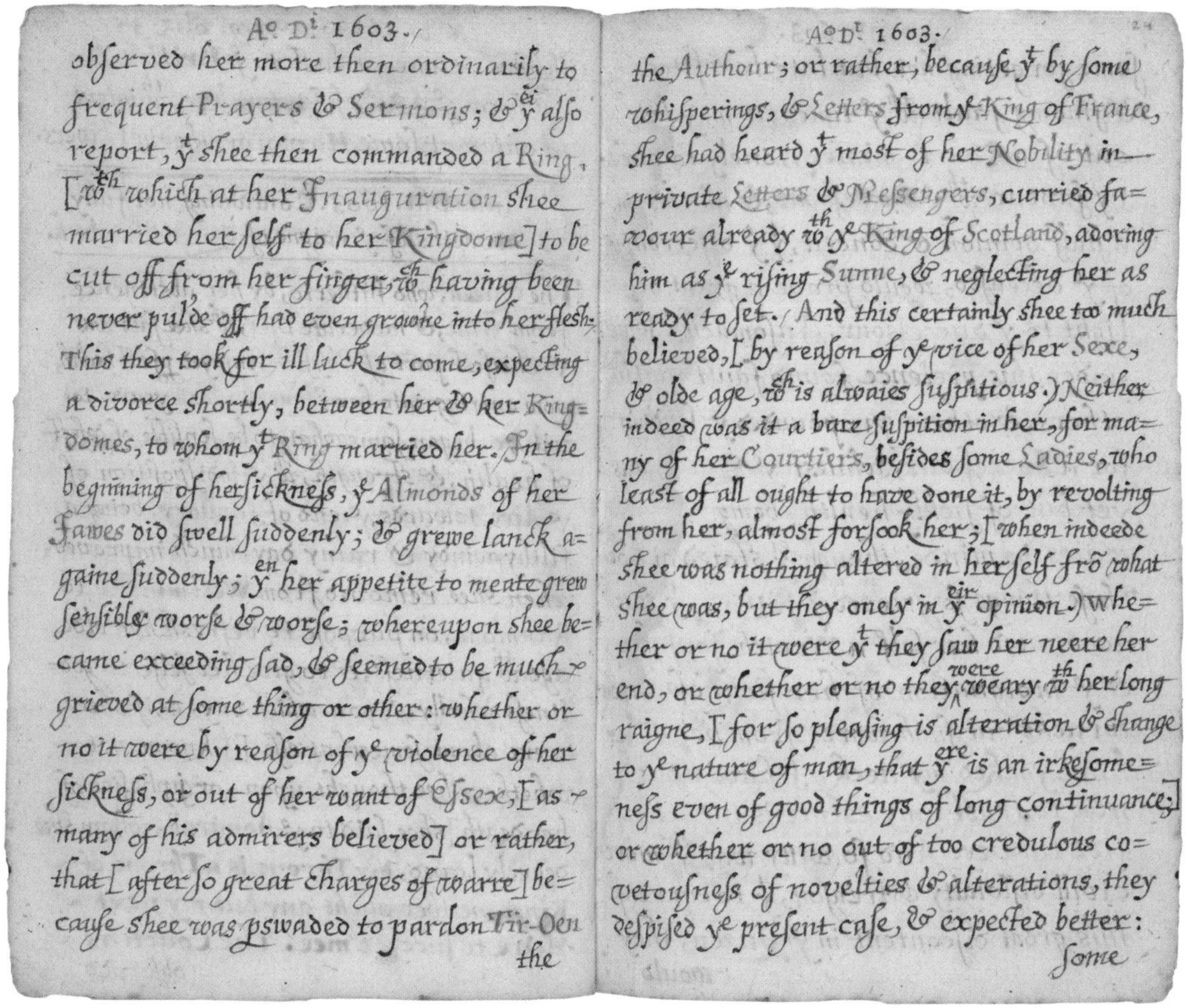
Ao. Di. 1603.
observed her more then ordinarily to
frequent Prayers & Sermons; & yei also
report, yt shee then commanded a Ring,
[wth which at her Inauguration shee
married her self to her Kingdome] to be
cut off from her finger, wch having been
never pulde off had even growne into her flesh.
This they took for ill luck to come, expecting
a divorce shortly, between her & her King=
domes, to whom yt Ring married her. In the
beginning of her sicknes, ye Almonds of her
Jawes did swell suddenly; & grewe lanck a=
gaine suddenly; yen her appetite to meate grew
sensibly worse & worse; whereupon shee be=
came exceeding sad, & seemed to be much
grieved at some thing or other: whether or
no it were by reason of ye violence of her
sicknes, or out of her want of Essex, [as
many of his admirers believed] or rather,
that [after so great charges of warre] be=
cause shee was pswaded to pardon Tir-Oen
the

Ao. Di. 1603.
the Authour; or rather, because yt by some
whisperings, & Letters from ye King of France,
shee had heard yt most of her Nobility in
private Letters & Messengers, curried fa=
vour already wth ye King of Scotland, adoring
him as ye rising Sunne, & neglecting her as
ready to set. And this certainly shee too much
believed, [by reason of ye vice of her Sexe,
& olde age, wch is alwaies suspitious.) Neither
indeed was it a bare suspition in her, for ma=
ny of her Courtiers, besides some Ladies, who
least of all ought to have done it, by revolting
from her, almost forsook her; [when indeede
shee was nothing altered in her self fro what
shee was, but they onely in yeir opinion.) Whe=
ther or no it were yt they saw her neere her
end, or whether or no they were weary wth her long
raigne, [for so pleasing is alteration & change
to ye nature of man, that yere is an irksome=
ness even of good things of long continuance]
or whether or no out of too credulous co=
vetousness of novelties & alterations, they
despised ye present case, & expected better:
Some

FIGURE 9.8 Historical extracts [manuscript] (c. 1625), fol. 23v–24r. Folger Shelf Mark X.d.393.

The image of James as sun king was not to everyone's liking. Certainly it failed to warm his predecessor on the throne, Elizabeth I. She was notoriously stingy with new noble titles, much to the resentment of many who had done her great service and expected social elevation as their reward. Nervously, she suspected that James would be less parsimonious with honors and so undermine her control of court in her last years. As reported by an anonymous court observer (fig. 9.8), the aged queen had "heard [tha]t most of her Nobility in Private Letters & Messengers, curried favour already w[i]th [th]e King of Scotland, adoring him as [th]e rising Sunne, & neglecting her as ready to set."[42]

These fears proved somewhat prescient. The new king would in time radically alter the face of aristocratic Britain.

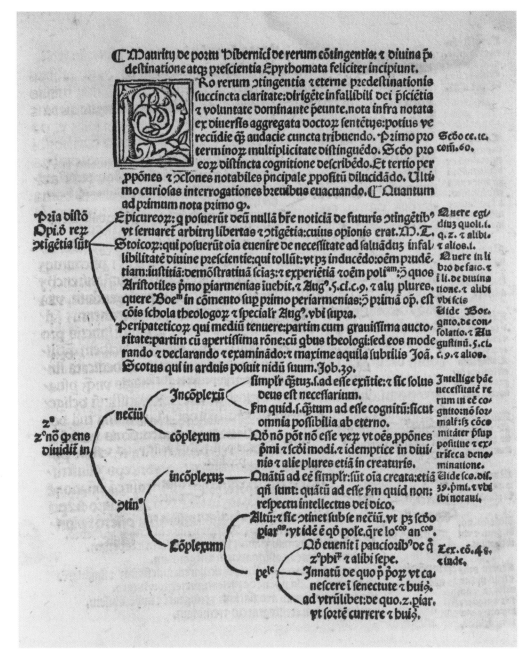

Figure 10.1 Maurice O'Fihely (d. 1513). *Enchyridion fidei*
(Venice: Boneto Locatelli, 1509), sig. A3r. Folger Shelf Mark 259-114q.

10
FLIGHT(S) OF THE EARLS: IRISH NOBLES IN ROME AND ENGLAND

ESPITE HIS BEST INTENTIONS, James was unable to unite his divergent nobility, and he helped provoke the Gaelic nobility's pursuit of closer ties with mainland Europe. These ties had always been in place; Irish intellectuals, for example, traced Gaelic roots to legendary ancestors from prehistoric Spain. Indeed, one of the arguments for Spanish aid during the Nine Years' War was the supposed blood connection between the two peoples. It thus became an imperative of family honor for Spain to help O'Neill resist Tudor rule. Whatever these fictive kinship links, Maurice O'Fihely's *Enchyridion Fidei* (1509; fig. 10.1)—one of the earliest printed books by an Irish writer—is a material reminder that Irish elite connections to continental political, ecclesiastical, and intellectual circles were of long standing.

O'Fihely, eventual Archbishop of Tuam, County Galway, taught scholastic philosophy to university students in Padua and published the book in nearby Venice. The *Enchyridion* is dedicated to the eighth Earl of Kildare, whose house became a vital center of learning in the Pale under him and his successors in the sixteenth century.

Other Irish intellectuals on the Continent provoked discord, given that these writers aimed to garner broader European support for local Irish struggles. The religious and political exile Richard Stanyhurst (see pages 19 and 24) wrote works in Latin that promoted both the

Catholic Counter-Reformation and Irish independence from England. His life of St. Patrick, *De Vita S. Patricii* (Antwerp, 1587; see fig. 10.2), for example, is dedicated in bold terms to the war hero and Catholic governor of the Spanish Netherlands, Alexander Farnese, Duke of Parma. Stanyhurst continued to agitate for the pan-Catholic cause well into the seventeenth century. Particularly vitriolic was Philip O'Sullivan Beare's *Historiae Catholicae Iberniae Compendium* (Lisbon, 1621; see fig. 10.3), which was intended to convince the Spanish monarchy that England's regime was hell-bent on suppressing true religion, controlling the island, and killing off the nobility.

As things turned out, Irish lords did not welcome continental reinforcements after the disasters of Smerwick (1580) and Kinsale (1601); rather, they would set sail for Catholic Europe themselves. The year 1607 marks one of the most poignant moments in Irish history: the so-called Flight of the Earls, when the Ulster lords Hugh O'Neill, Earl of Tyrone, and Rory O'Donnell, Earl of Tyrconnell—so recently aligned with the crown—fled to the Continent in the face of royal suspicions that they plotted further rebellion. This event inspired poetic laments for the passing of the old ways, such as Aindrias mac Marcuis's "Anocht is uaigneach Éire":

DE VITA
S. PATRICII,
HIBERNIÆ
APOSTOLI,
LIBRI II.

Nunc primùm in lucem editi,

Auctore

RICHARDO STANIHVRSTO

DVBLINIENSI.

ANTVERPIÆ,

Ex officina Christophori Plantini,

Architypographi Regij.

M. D. LXXXVII.

14

DOMINI
PHILIPPI OSVLLEVANI
BEARRI IBERNI,
TOMI. I. LIBER. II.

De Purgatorio Diui Patritij.

 Vperest adhuc omnium memorabilium rerum Iberniæ maxima, de qua principe loco fuisset agendum, nisi seorsim hic fusius enarrandam esse duxissem. Ea est Diui Patritij Purgatorium.

CAPVT. I.

Promittit author se relaturum historiam hominis, qui à Purgatorio Diui Patritij reuersus est.

IN Purgatorio Diui Patritij multorum hominum animas ob peccata, quæ corporibus inclusæ admiserunt, cruciari, compertum est. Vnde quam falsus, & impius sit error eorum, qui peccatores homines, sed in gratia Dei obeuntes Purgatorium manere negant, hoc vnum satis est argumento : præterquam quod diuinis litteris apertissime colligitur. Ego quidem legi, & in quodam Ibernico libro, & apud Diuum Dionysium Carthusianum in *Liber Ibernic. D. Dion. Carthus.*

(*left*) FIGURE 10.2 Richard Stanyhurst (1547–1618). *De vita S. Patricii* (Antwerp: Christophe Plantin, 1587), title page, Folger Shelf Mark BX4700.P3 S8 1587 Cage.

(*above*) FIGURE 10.3 Philip O'Sullivan Beare (1590?–1660?). *Historiae catholicae Iberniae* (Lisbon: Petro Crasbecckio, 1621), 14. Folger Shelf Mark DA910.O7 Cage.

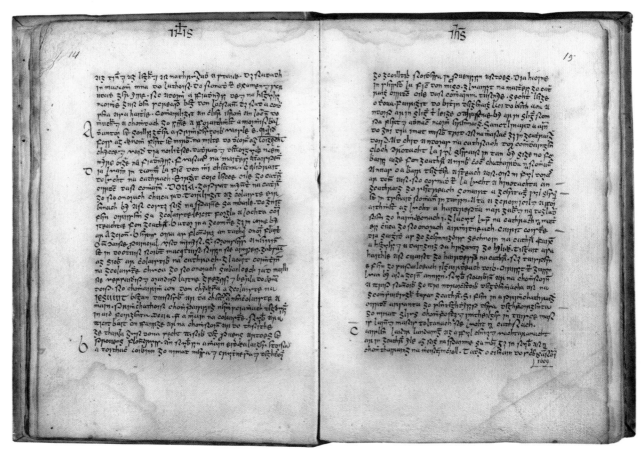

FIGURE 10.4 Tadhg Ó Cianáin (d. 1614). *Diary of the Flight of Earls* [manuscript] (c. 1609), fol. 14v–15r. Courtesy of University College, Dublin.

Anocht is uaigneach Éire,
do-bheir fógra a fírfréimhe;
gruaidhe a fear 'sa fionnbhan flioch,
treabh is iongnadh go uaignioch.[43]

Tonight Ireland is desolate,
The banishment of her true race
Has left wet-cheeked her men and her fair women;
Strange that such a dwelling-place should be desolate.[44]

Over the years, these verses have led many—scholars and the general populace—to see the "Flight" as signaling the end of the Gaelic world. Recent research, though, has shown that the earls did not intend their exile to be permanent. Instead, they traveled to the courts of Catholic Europe and the Vatican seeking support to return and reclaim their authority in Ireland.

Our only contemporary account of their trip from Ulster to Rome is contained in Tadhg Ó Cianáin's Irish-language diary (fig. 10.4). The diarist was of a storied bardic family from Fermanagh who traditionally

FIGURE 10.5 Hugh O'Neill (in background) in Rome, detail from an Italian fresco (16th century). Photo courtesy of Hiram Morgan.

78

produced *ollúna* for the ruling Maguires. Ó Cianáin's text paints a very different picture of the journey from that of mac Marcuis's lament "Anocht is uaigneach Éire." It depicts the Irish lords hosted with honor in major Catholic cities and courts of the Continent. At the Irish College in Douai—seat of Gaelic Counter-Reformation priests and intellectuals in exile and the home of a printing press with Gaelic type—"the communities of the colleges received them respectfully and kindly, delivering for them verses and speeches in Latin, Greek, and English."[45] In Rome, the pope himself gave them presents of "a silver basket, a pair of white doves, a golden bottle full of wine, [and] a gilded loaf of bread."[46] The earls' inclusion in Roman politics and society is visually confirmed by a recently identified portrait of Hugh O'Neill in the papal court (fig. 10.5). The gray-bearded O'Neill sits beside the Spanish ambassador and behind the pope during the canonization of St. Francesca Romana.

O'Neill and O'Donnell's journey to Rome was not the only flight of Irish nobility. O'Sullivan Beare's uncle Donal Cam O'Sullivan Beare (see page 61) was defeated by crown forces after the Battle of Kinsale and in 1605 left for Spain, where he became Count of Bearehaven in the Spanish nobility. The commoner Thomas Carew (Carve), of Gaelic cultural background and descended from the Butlers of Ormond, wrote an itinerary of his travels to the Continent after 1633, the highly popular *Itinerarium* (Mainz, 1639; fig. 10.6). Dedicated to both the twelfth Earl and the Countess of Ormond, it focuses extensively on the Thirty Years' War, which Carew witnessed firsthand. The book is especially noted for its account of the death of General Wallenstein, assassinated with the help of Carew's Irish employer, Colonel Walter Butler.

The Earl of Ormond would himself enter exile in France with his master King Charles II during the Cromwellian Interregnum (1649–60). The earls of Clanricard and Thomond also flew from their ancestral homes, although only as far as the Stuart courts of London and Dublin. Richard Burke, fourth Earl of Clanricard, is the great

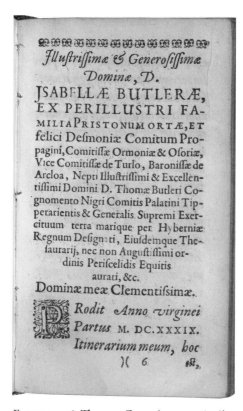

FIGURE 10.6 Thomas Carve (1590–1672?).
Itinerarium (London: Nicholas Heyll,
1639), sig.) (6r. Folger Shelf Mark
D915.C29 1639 Cage.

FIGURE 10.7 The west entrance of the estate of Earl of Clanricard, Somerhill, Kent.
Published in *Country Life* magazine, September 9, 1922.

79

success story of noble integration in the early Stuart period. Numerous English and Scottish newcomers would receive titles in Ireland under James (see chapter 12). But this Old English noble from Galway managed elevation in the other direction: He picked up a title in the English peerage, being named Earl of St. Albans in 1628.

Clanricard would also be honored with inclusion in the Order of the Garter, and prove a regular in heraldic displays and presentations. In figure 10.7 we see the earl's estate in Kent, Somerhill, a property bought in part with wealth and connections realized through his marriage to Fran-

ces Walsingham, daughter of Elizabeth I's counselor Francis Walsingham and widow of both Sir Philip Sidney and the second Earl of Essex.

Clanricard paid close attention to his Irish estates as well. He was in constant contact with his agents there and talked of returning to Connacht to live. Like his former foes O'Neill and O'Donnell on the Continent, however, Clanricard spent the rest of his life away from the land of his birth. None of the three intended a one-way flight from Ireland, but the result for each was permanent exile among the nobility of other nations.

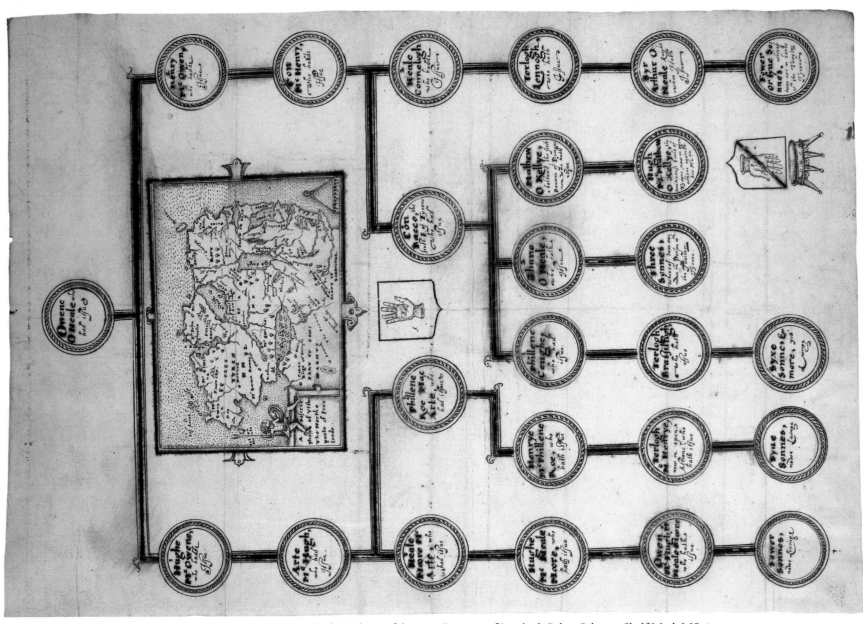

FIGURE 11.1 Carew Manuscript. Gaelic Pedigree, fol. 139a. Courtesy of Lambeth Palace Library, Shelf Mark MS 635.

11

THE "END OF THE GAELIC ORDER"?:
THE ULSTER PLANTATION

Gonzalo. Had I plantation of this isle, my lord—
Antonio. He'd sow't with nettle seed
Sebastian. Or docks, or mallows.
Gonzalo. And were the King on't, what would I do?[47]

"FLIGHT" OR NOT, the Ulster earls' abandonment of their ancestral lands would have radical consequences for the north of Ireland. The crown read this action as proof of renewed machinations with the Spanish against the English state. This, then, was treason, and the government claimed the ancestral territories of the O'Neills, the O'Donnells, and the Maguires as its own. Thus began in 1609 the greatest of English colonization schemes in Ireland: the Ulster Plantation.

The plantation was larger than any of its Tudor predecessors. It introduced on an unprecedented scale British law and investment along with English and Presbyterian Scots settlers into the region, which was previously deemed the most uncivil and intractable in Ireland. The crown's claim to what had been to this point the least Anglicized part of Ireland is made visually manifest in a "political" genealogy that shows the rise and fall of the O'Neill earls of Tyrone (fig. 11.1). There is no other pedigree like this known to exist: Not only does it chart the transformation of Irish chiefs to English earls—

notice the circle indicating "Con Bacco" as first Earl of Tyrone—and represent their eventual "open rebellion" by picturing the earl's coronet (the heraldic symbol appropriate to the title) turned upside down, but it also displays their heraldic symbol, the red hand, and their traditional lands now marked for colonization by the Stuart monarch James I. The fall of the old nobility in Ulster would pave the way for new noble titles to sprout from those lands.

As in Munster in the 1580s and '90s but with better planning and results, at least from the crown's perspective, the Ulster Plantation project (see fig. 11.2) attracted able thinkers and opportunistic administrators. The courtier-poet Sir John Davies, who served as Speaker of the Irish House of Commons and Solicitor General of Ireland, was one of the plantation's key architects. His book *A Discoverie of the True Causes why Ireland was Never Entirely Subdued* (1612; see fig. 11.3) analyzes Ireland's problems and colonial reforms. Like many New English before him, Davies saw in his writing a chance for patronage. Famously, he claimed Ireland to be so peaceful that

[w]e may conceive an hope that the next generation will be in tongue and heart and every way else become English; so as there will be no difference or distinction but the Irish sea betwixt us.[48]

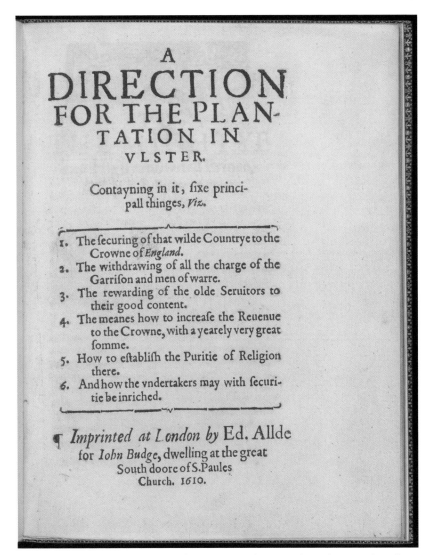

FIGURE 11.2 *A direction for the plantation in Ulster.* London: Thomas Blenerhasset, 1610), title page. Courtesy of Beinecke Rare Book and Manuscript Library, Yale University, Shelf Mark Beinecke no. 1974 631.

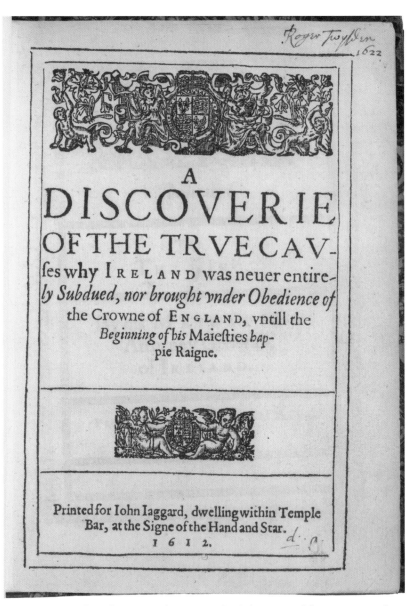

FIGURE 11.3 Sir John Davies (1569–1626). *A discoverie of the true causes why Ireland was never entirely Subdued* ([London: William Jaggard], 1612), title page. Folger Shelf Mark STC 6348.

A man of law and letters, Davies credited Ireland's newly realized civility to James I's success at overseeing the introduction of common law to the realm. As we have also noted, in the epigram on page 53, he believed in the use of the sword before the biblical word in "barbarous" circumstances.

Colonial themes are explicitly presented to a London audience in Shakespeare's *The Tempest* (c. 1610–11; published 1623; fig. 11.4), which was first staged in London while Ulster was being carved up among British investors. Caliban and his mother, Sycorax, have taken over a magical island somewhere in the Mediterranean (although mention of the "vexed Bermoothes" brings Bermuda to mind), where they are accused of tyrannical, barbaric, and incompetent behavior, and are themselves pushed aside by incoming Europeans. One of these Europeans, the wise counselor Gonzalo, fantasizes about becoming "king" of the island and there creating a "plantation," so as "[t]'excel the Golden Age":

> All things in common nature should produce
> Without sweat or endeavor; treason, felony,
> Sword, pike, knife, gun, or need of any engine,
> Would I not have; but nature should bring forth
> Of its own kind all foison, all abundance,
> To feed my innocent people.[49]

Gonzalo, faced with a colonial opportunity, wants to become king of a fantastic realm; his lord, Alonso, king of Naples, is despondent and interested only in whether his son and heir, Ferdinand, survived the shipwreck. One stands to gain from the new land, one to lose. The contrast between dream and reality for these two lords could not be more stark.

FIGURE 11.4 William Shakespeare (1564–1616). *Mr William Shakespeares comedies, histories, & tragedies* (London: Isaac Iaggard & Ed. Blount, 1623), first page of *The Tempest*. Folger Shelf Mark STC 22273 Fo. 1 no. 75.

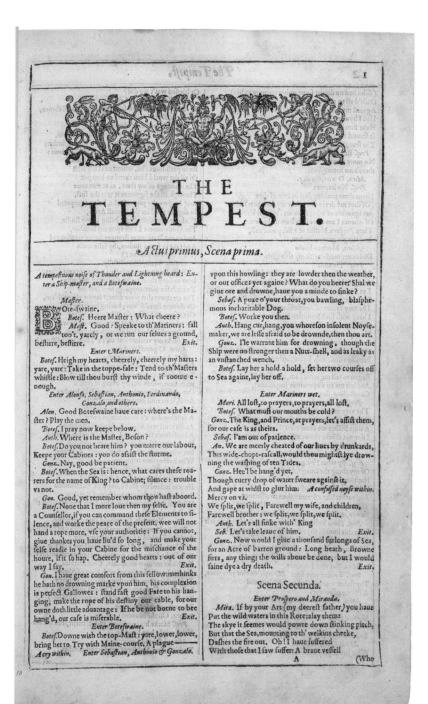

83

FIGURE 12.1 Peter Paul Rubens (1577–1640). Portrait of George Villiers (1592–1628), first Duke of Buckingham (17th century). Courtesy of Palazzo Pitti/The Bridgeman Art Library.

12
Land and Law:
The new nobility

CHANGES IN LANDOWNERSHIP were not the only revolutionary outcome of the Ulster lords' defeat and exile. Changed, too, was the social landscape, as the Stuarts worked assiduously to fashion a new nobility, like-minded and loyal. There was great pressure from below for the creation of titles in all the realms: What Elizabeth had refused to do it was hoped James would. And he did, with profligacy. What began as a good thing in the eyes of elites in all three kingdoms—the elevation of the loyal and deserving—quickly turned sour as the regime handed out titles to favorites and sold off more of them to raise money for the royal coffers. The crown even created a new title of minor nobility, the baronet, which could be peddled to social climbers with deep pockets, a development that scandalized the "ancient" nobility.

The use of Ulster land as the basis for new titles was equally crass. The King's favorite, George Villiers, Duke of Buckingham (fig. 12.1), oversaw this market in titles, and his underlings sold them to the highest bidder. Purchasers typically never saw the Irish lands on which their "nobility" depended, let alone took up residence there. A particularly sordid example is that of Sir William Pope, created Earl of Down in 1628. Pope was an Oxfordshire man of gentry stock. He wanted elevation to the peerage and knew the easiest way to realize that goal was by purchase of an Irish title. He entrusted his son Thomas to make the arrangements and gave clear instructions as to how much he was willing to spend (preferably £2,250 and no higher than £2,500). Thomas wrote back from London informing the earl that an Irish agent suggested titles linked to Granard and Lucan, and though he himself could not find them on any map, he assured his father that others said they did in fact exist.

The traditional communal links between noble title and local leadership were clearly of no interest to Pope. Eventually he would wrangle a title linked, as his son Thomas put it, to "a countie [i.e., Down] and not any privat towne."[50] Yet Pope would never set foot in Ireland; the title was merely to boost his place in English society. We may therefore question how "noble" this process was. Pope did hand down his noble

FIGURE 12.2 Effigies of William Pope, Earl of Downe (1595–1640), and his wife, All Saints Church, Wroxton, Oxfordshire.
Photo courtesy of Simon Marsden/The Bridgeman Art Library.

86

status to posterity: His elegant funerary monument (fig. 12.2) is as striking now as it was in the seventeenth century. His effigy lies in stately repose, bearing his earl's coronet.

The most famous, or notorious, example of the meteoric rise of a commoner into the ranks of the aristocracy in this period is a man who made his initial fortune in the Munster Plantation prior to James's accession: Richard Boyle.

A commoner from Kent, Boyle used land speculation in Munster, political connections in Dublin and London, and advantageous marriages for him and his family to amass one of the greatest fortunes in

Britain. He could thus afford, in 1620, the forty-five hundred pounds it cost to create an earldom (of Cork) for himself and a viscountcy (of Dungarvan) for his son. On the death of his second wife, Catherine Fenton, in 1630 he memorialized her and cemented his and his family's status in the eyes of metropolitan Dublin by erecting an immense funerary monument in St. Patrick's Cathedral (fig. 12.3). Lord Deputy Wentworth sneered that it was Cork's "pedigree" and lobbied Charles I for permission to have it dismantled.

The Boyles were not the only family from Kent who used Ireland as a leg up in the social hierarchy. The Taylors of Shadoxhurst were of longstanding gentry stock. During Elizabeth's reign, one of the sons took up plantation land in County Cavan and thus started an Irish line to the family. Even the main line remaining in Kent bore an Irish stamp: In 1664, Thomas Taylor made the jump from gentry to nobility by purchasing a baronetage. This type of title, the lowest in the heraldic hierarchy, was newly created by King James and the Duke of Buckingham as a way to make money from the demand, and willingness to pay, for status elevation. The traditional arms of the family—two boars' heads—were thus joined by the red hand of Ulster (see fig. 12.4). A further Irish echo to this pedigree is its mention of "gavelkind." This was a curiosity in England, a system of partible inheritance (that is, distribution of land among heirs) that ran counter to the dominant practice of primogeniture (by which all land stayed with the eldest son). When English officials and planters witnessed how Irish lords divided their lands among heirs, they termed it "gavelkind." Spenser and Davies, for example, in their condemnations of Gaelic gavelkind, described it as among the "savagery" to be eliminated in both realms. Against the claims of these parvenu nobles, ancient

FIGURE 12.3 Boyle's funerary monument, St. Patrick's Cathedral, Dublin.
Photo courtesy of St. Patrick's Cathedral.

88

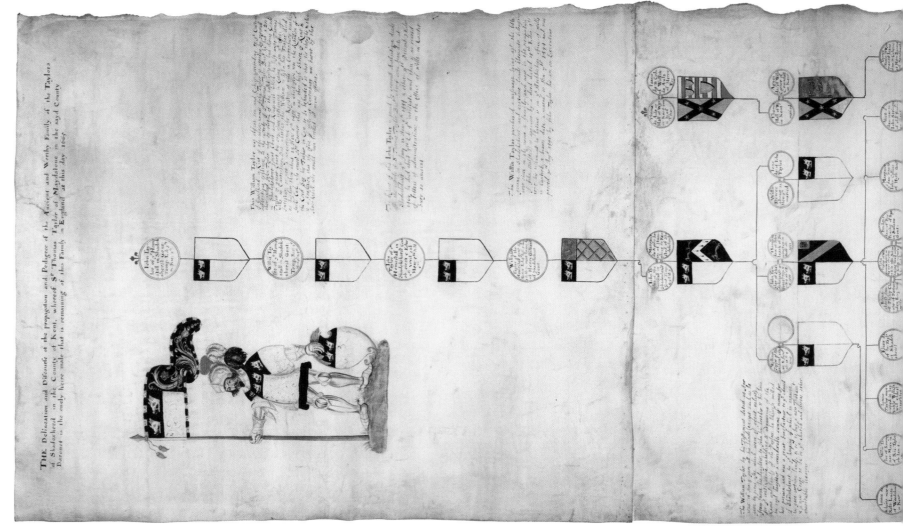

FIGURE 12.4 Pedigree of the Taylor family, Shadoxhurst, Kent
[manuscript], 1665. Folger Shelf Mark Z.e.41.

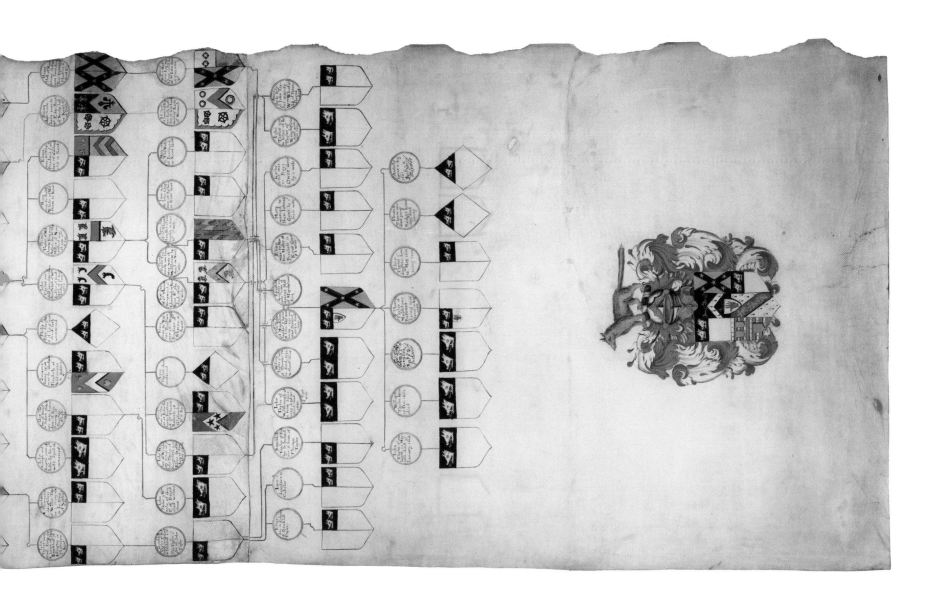

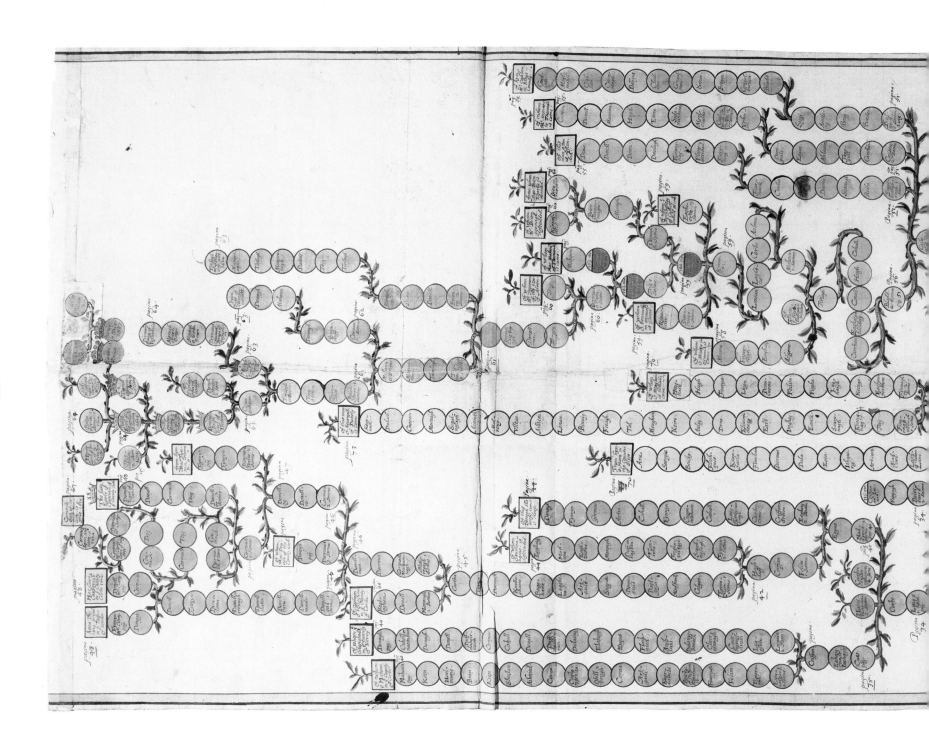

90

lords such as Donogh O'Brien, fourth Earl of Thomond, commissioned colorful book pedigrees to highlight their social legitimacy. Like Cork, Thomond's aristocratic seat was in the provinces; consequently, he was eager to stamp his authority on metropolitan Dublin. On the one hand, this was accomplished through political position: He became a leader in the Irish House of Lords and was closely connected to James and his court. On the other hand, he too could deploy the heraldic arts. Reproduced here is a foldout pedigree of all the Gaelic aristocratic families as they descended from Spanish lords and, back in the mists of time, from a "noble Grecian." Included in the fourth Earl of Thomond's own book pedigree (fig. 12.5), it was intended to place the O'Brien chieftain's lineage within its broader historical and social contexts. No simple tracing of the O'Briens alone, this massive book—something to be displayed to visitors—contained a list of Irish high kings and their lineal origins and tracked the histories of all the noble Gaels and their political fortunes. The O'Neill line, for example, ends with Tyrone's "open rebellion" and his arms tilted upside down. Family trees were never simply about families.

91

FIGURE 12.5 Thomond Pedigree [manuscript] (16th century). Courtesy of the National Library of Ireland, Shelf Mark G.o.158.

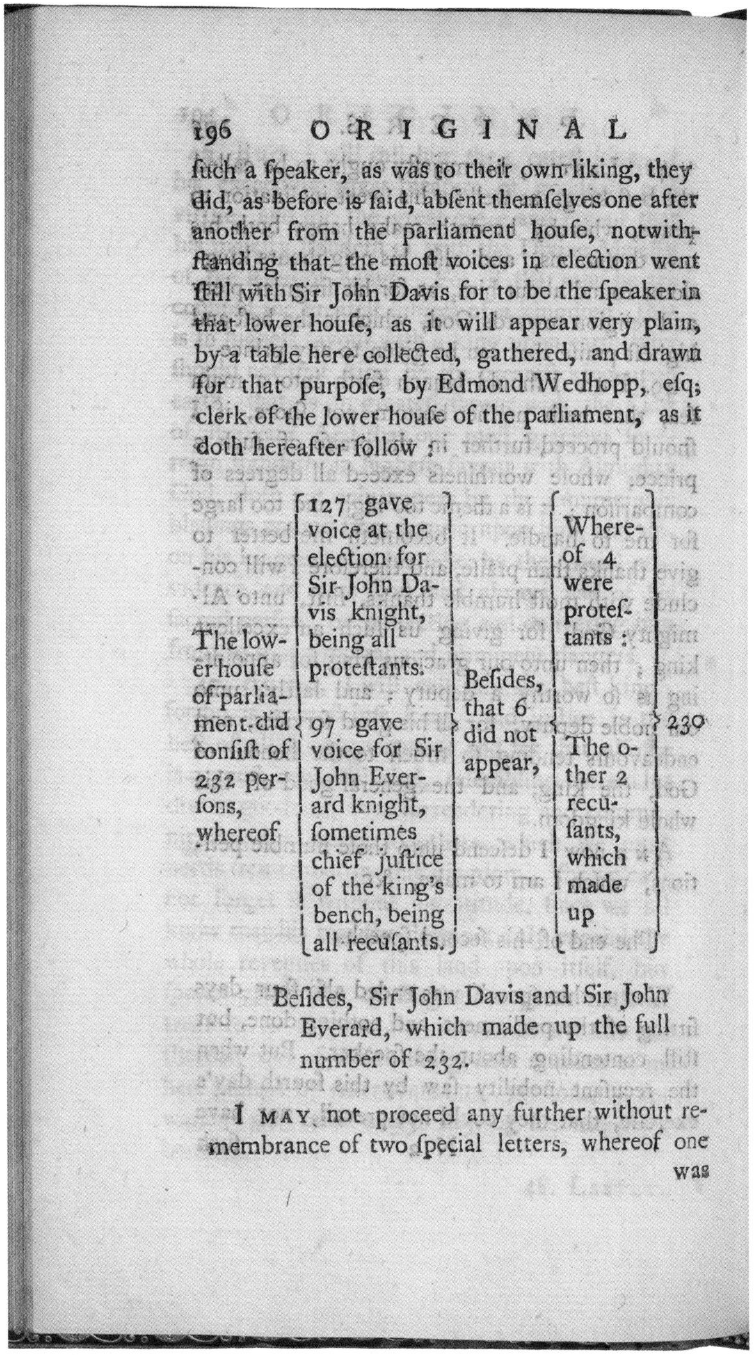

196 ORIGINAL

ſuch a ſpeaker, as was to their own liking, they did, as before is ſaid, abſent themſelves one after another from the parliament houſe, notwithſtanding that the moſt voices in election went ſtill with Sir John Davis for to be the ſpeaker in that lower houſe, as it will appear very plain, by a table here collected, gathered, and drawn for that purpoſe, by Edmond Wedhopp, eſq; clerk of the lower houſe of the parliament, as it doth hereafter follow:

The lower houſe of parliament did conſiſt of 232 perſons, whereof	127 gave voice at the election for Sir John Davis knight, being all proteſtants.	Beſides, that 6 did not appear,	Whereof 4 were proteſtants:	230
	97 gave voice for Sir John Everard knight, ſometimes chief juſtice of the king's bench, being all recuſants.		The other 2 recuſants, which made up	

Beſides, Sir John Davis and Sir John Everard, which made up the full number of 232.

I MAY not proceed any further without remembrance of two ſpecial letters, whereof one was

FIGURE 12.6 *Desiderata curiosa Hibernica* (Dublin: David Hay, 1772), 196. Folger Shelf Mark DA905.L8 v. 1 Cage.

Old English nobles also bristled at the pretensions of new men such as Cork. As described in the *Desiderata Curiosa Hibernica* (fig. 12.6), an eighteenth-century collection of important political papers related to sixteenth- and seventeenth-century English–Irish relations, some of the Old English used the opening of the 1613–14 Parliament in Dublin as an opportunity to express their displeasure over matters of precedence. During the ceremonial march to services at nearby Christ Church Cathedral, in the administrative heart of Dublin, a number of them, in full view of the city's populace, stepped out of the procession in protest at having to walk behind more recently ennobled delegates. The Irish lord deputy Arthur Chichester, begging them not to dishonor the procession, was helpless to stop them. Eventually he complained to the King, who sent a delegation to settle these matters of honor. The delegates, however, only fell to squabbling among themselves over precedence—who would sit where at the council table while it was in session—and thus added mockery to what was already scandalous behavior by the local nobility.

Religion might also play a role in dividing sides. Figure 12.6 shows a chart of the vote over Attorney General Sir John Davies's bid to be Speaker of the House of Commons, a vote that broke along confessional lines: that is, Catholic vs. Protestant.

Old English nobles and their writers were also keen to ensure that their status was respected in England. In his manuscript treatise on English–Irish relations, *Ireland's Comfort* (1629; fig. 12.7), John Cusack made apparent the historical and legal reasons why a noble title under the crown was just as meaningful regardless of what Stuart realm in which it was held. Here we read that "a nobleman of England may be free from areast for debt in Ireland, & a nobleman of Ireland may

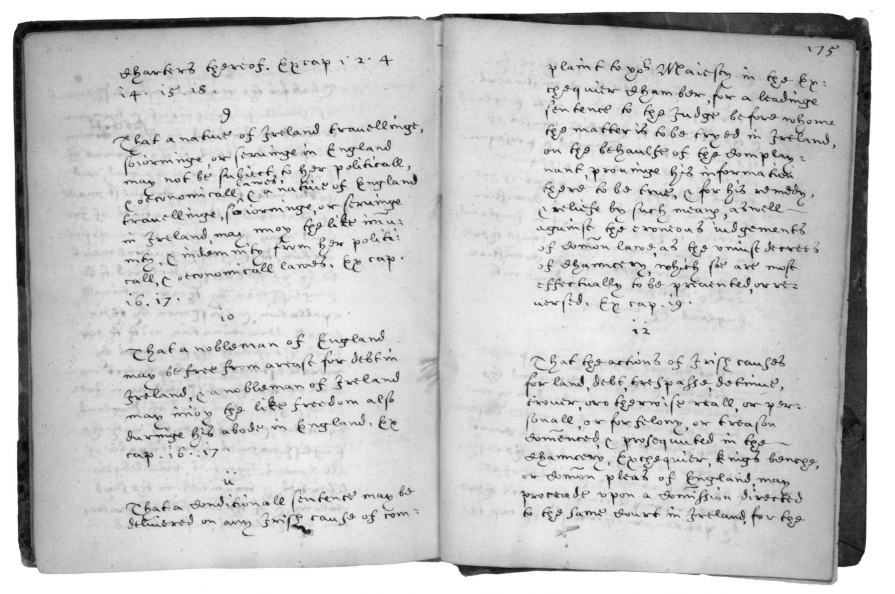

FIGURE 12.7 John Cusack (17th century). *Ireland's comfort* [manuscript] ([1629?]), fol. 174v–175r. Folger Shelf Mark G.a.10.

enjoy the like freedom also during his abode in England."[51] The comforts of Ireland, then, were to follow Irish nobles wherever they moved within the British Isles, and Irish elites were to enjoy the privileges of rank and not be treated as inferior subjects when crossing borders . . . at least in theory.

Interest in comparative status and noble lineage was shared by no less a personage than Edmund Tilney, Master of Revels for Elizabeth I. Tilney's great book of European aristocratic families (c. 1597–1601; fig. 12.8) contains short histories and colored coats of arms of the major families: Gaelic, Old English, and New English, including various branches of the Butler, Lacey, O'Conor, O'Brien, and Burke families. Organized by province, the text includes short histories of the major resident nobles. In the struggle for social legitimacy, battle lines crisscrossed the Irish Sea.

The struggle for social legitimacy also crossed cultural and "ethnic" boundaries, as demonstrated in the life and fortunes of Randal mac Sorley MacDonnell, first Earl of Antrim. MacDonnell was a Scotsman and client of the King's favorite, the Earl of Buckingham. Related to Hugh O'Neill, Earl of Tyrone, MacDonnell fought on the rebel side in the Nine Years' War. His later reconciliation with the Stuart crown, however, was complete. Although a committed Catholic, his money and connections ensured his creation as Earl of Antrim in 1618. In Dunluce on the Antrim coast, he would extensively renovate, in renaissance fashion, an imposing castle dramatically perched on ocean cliffs (see page xiii). More dramatic still was the cultural integration MacDonnell engineered, for in spite of being a new noble, elevated to the peerage for cash at the hands of Buckingham, MacDonnell did not turn his back entirely on Gaelic culture and its arbiters of status. The *ollamh* (that is, bard-historian) Fear Flatha Ó Gnímh constructed a lineage for the new earl, thus helping to legitimize him as a local Lord. The Gaelic learned class put their skills to welcoming not only their new King, but also his new nobles.

FIGURE 12.8 Edmund Tilney (d. 1610). *Topographical descriptions, regiments, and policies* [manuscript] (c. 1597–c. 1601), fol. 342v–343r. Folger Shelf Mark V.b.182.

Irlande

Ormond

Buttler

Meth

Conagh

Lacie

Conagh

o = Connor

Burch

Irlande

343

Burch Earle of Clanricard

Obryen

Thomond.

Ulster.

95

FIGURE 13.1 Edmund Spenser (1552?–99). *A view of the [present] state of Ireland,* in Edmund Campion (1540–81). *Two histories of Ireland* (Dublin: Society of Stationers, 1633), title page. Folger Shelf Mark STC 25067a copy 2 part 3.

13
STUART DUBLIN,
C. 1603–41

TUDOR DUBLIN (see chapter 2) was a very different provincial capital from that under the Stuarts. Military "pacification" of Ireland and the attendant process of "Anglicization," as envisioned by New English policymakers such as Edmund Spenser, Richard Beacon, and Sir John Davies, reshaped the social, cultural, and political landscapes of the city. The result, however, was not always an increased intolerance.

In 1633, the historian and court politico Sir James Ware published three histories of Ireland written under the Tudors but never previously in print. One was by Edmund Campion, the eventual Catholic martyr, who wrote it in Dublin in 1570 under the patronage of Sir Henry Sidney. The book formed the basis of Stanyhurst's Irish history in Holinshed's *Chronicles* (1577); Stanyhurst was Campion's pupil (see page 19). Another was by the Protestant Church of Ireland clergyman Meredith Hanmer, a staunch opponent of Campion's religiosity. The third, *A View of the [Present] State of Ireland* (c. 1596; fig. 13.1), was by a layman, the poet and administrator Edmund Spenser.

This curious mixture of writers demonstrated Ware's tolerant attitude toward competing ideologies in the name of scholarship, although we may wonder if that tolerance was absolute, given the notable absence of a native Irish point of view. This was not for lack of material: Irish history was actively being written and published in

Ireland and on the Continent in the 1620s and '30s, most famously in Philip O'Sullivan Beare's *Historiae Catholicae Iberniae Compendium*, published in Lisbon in 1621 (see page 75), in Geoffrey Keating's *Foras Feasa ar Éirinn*, c. 1634, and in the manuscript *Annals of the Four Masters*, compiled in Donegal while James Ware was working on his volume on the opposite side of the island, in the early 1630s. Whatever his sources, Ware showed a desire for social harmony not seen in the works of Spenser and Davies. Reflecting how conditions had improved since the Nine Years' War—the backdrop against which Spenser penned his tract—Ware edited out many of the planter and poet's harsher comments on the Old English. Where Spenser had written "the Lordes and Chief men wax so barbarous and bastardlike," Ware softened it to read "the Lords and cheife men degenerate." More generally, he simply deleted many uses of aggressive descriptors such as "barbarous," "salvage," and "wilde."[52]

The book was dedicated to the incoming Lord Deputy, Thomas Wentworth (later Earl of Strafford). From gentry stock in the north of England, Wentworth rose during Charles I's reign as a result of his intellectual and administrative abilities; he also supported protecting and strengthening the royal prerogative. Variously a member of Parliament, a sheriff, and eventually Lord President of the Council of the North (in England), he was nonetheless never a martial man. Yet upon

FIGURE 13.2 Sir Anthony van Dyck (1599–1641). Portrait of Thomas Wentworth (1593–1641), Earl of Strafford (1633–36), oil on canvas. Courtesy of Private Collection/The Bridgeman Art Library.

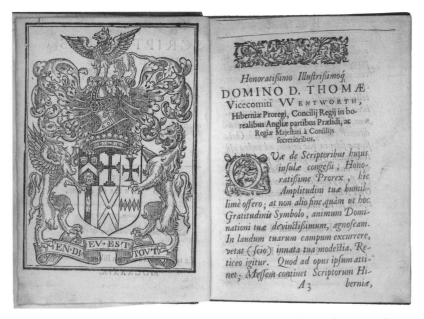

FIGURE 13.3 Sir James Ware (1594–1666). *De scriptoribus Hiberniae. Libri duo* (Dublin: Society of Booksellers, 1639), sig. A2v–A3r. Folger Shelf Mark STC 25066 copy 2.

accepting Charles's nomination to be Lord Deputy of Ireland, Wentworth posed in armor beside a docile Irish wolfhound (fig. 13.2). The imagery was as unmistakable as it was incongruous, given the man: The pacified and planted Ireland was firmly under the crown, and even the Wentworths of the world would take up the sword to "civilize" the island should its inhabitants prefer to bark rather than heel.

Despite Ware's bowdlerization of Spenser's original, his own writing was no less affected by colonial contexts than was Wentworth's armor portrait. His two-volume *De Scriptoribus Hiberniae* (1639; fig. 13.3) was a history of Irish writers, native and foreign, that intended to create a "loyal" genealogy of the written word in Ireland by appropriating the cultural past to crown ends. Among the writers within it are none other than Sir Henry Sidney and his son Sir Philip (see page 14), and, of course, Stanyhurst and Spenser. Ware also

FIGURE 13.4 Charles Brookings. Detail of Dublin Castle from map of Dublin (1728). Courtesy of the National Library of Ireland.

corresponded at length on Irish history with James Ussher, Archbishop of Armagh and Primate of Ireland, and did important antiquarian and archival work.

It should be pointed out that Ware was no mere dry and dusty scholar. He was also a member of Wentworth's council, Auditor General, and a fellow of Trinity College Dublin. No one in the regime knew more about Irish land and history. Thus, Ware's expertise was called upon to settle matters of precedence among quarreling nobles, and even to bolster claims for new plantations in Ireland's west. Knowledge truly equaled power in early Stuart Dublin.

Wentworth worked assiduously to make Dublin's culture and society worthy of the viceregal court. Arguably this was the most autonomous,

and therefore powerful, office under the English crown, and the new Lord Deputy took pains to make sure everyone knew it. In addition to overseeing repairs and renovations to Dublin Castle (fig. 13.4) — much of it in a terrible state of disrepair at his arrival — he gave express orders that no "Irish dress" be worn in presentation rooms: Those seeking audience with royal officials were to dress with English civility. Renaissance manners and courtliness were at home in Wentworth's Dublin, even if Gaelic culture was not.

Wentworth oversaw the establishment of the city's first theater, located in Werburgh Street, near Dublin Castle, and enticed the popular London playwright James Shirley to write for it. Shirley, like other newcomers, bet that he could parlay success in Dublin into greater

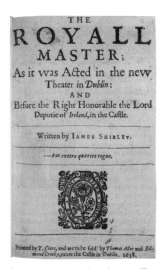

FIGURE 13.5 James Shirley (1596–1666). *The royall master* ([London]: Thomas Cotes, 1638), title page. Folger Shelf Mark STC 22454a copy 2.

(*right*) FIGURE 13.6 James Shirley (1596–1666). *St. Patrick for Ireland* (London: I. Raworth, 1640), title page. Folger Shelf Mark STC 22455 copy 1.

100

fame in London. He sought aristocratic patronage among those with connections to both cities. The resilience of the reduced Old English nobility is nowhere more obvious than in Shirley's dedication of a play, *The Royall Master* (1638; fig. 13.5), to George Fitzgerald, sixteenth Earl of Kildare, who spent much of his youth at court in London. The playwright, however, was careful to include an epilogue to his viceregal master, Wentworth. (As a curious aside, the seventeenth Earl of Kildare would be given the Christian name Wentworth. Wentworth Fitzgerald, seventeenth Earl of Kildare: a remarkable mixture of names among the nobility.)

Befitting his new patronage and location, Shirley penned a drama with an overtly Irish theme. *St. Patrick for Ireland* (1640; fig. 13.6) ends with Patrick converting the pagan king of Ireland to Christianity by virtue of defeating a raft of "creeping" snakes sent onstage by the evil sorcerer Archimagus (an echo of Archimago, Spenser's evil sorcerer in *The Faerie Queene*). Proclaims Patrick,

. . . all these can I
Approach, and without trembling, walk upon,
Play with their stings . . .
Hence, you frightful monsters,
Go hide, and bury your deformed heads
For ever in the sea; from this time be
This Iland free from beasts of venomous natures:
The Shepherd shall not be afraid hereafter,
To trust his eyes with sleep upon the hils,
The travellers shall have no suspition,
Or feare, to measure with his wearied limbs
The silent shades, but walk through everie brake,
Without more guard than his owne innocence.
The verie earth and wood shall have this blessing
(Above what other Christian Nations boast)
Although transported where these Serpents live
And multiply, one touch shall soone destroy 'em.[53]

St. Patrick's power, "transported where these Serpents live," foreshadows that of the government, which hoped to reform Ireland into a peaceful state "[a]bove what other Christian Nations boast."

Looking ahead, Shirley and his master Wentworth established a trend of Dublin-based, "noble"-minded theater that (like all other theater in the British realm) was suppressed during the republican Interregnum (1649–60) but revived with the Restoration (1660). At that time, Smock Alley Theatre in Dublin began staging plays written by, for example, Katherine Philips and Roger Boyle, first Earl of Orrery. Philips wrote the highly innovative *Pompey* (1663), a translation of a play by the Frenchman Corneille, and Orrery wrote and staged his own version of *Henry V* (1664), which focuses primarily on the English king's romance with the French princess Katherine: a peaceful theme for more peaceful times.

It seemed that Dublin in the 1620s and '30s was becoming the second city of the realms, boasting a viceregal court in full flower. Published in Dublin were such works of aristocratic leisure as Sir Philip Sidney's *Arcadia,* seen here in a revised edition from 1624 (fig. 13.7). This famous romance of errant princes and philosophizing shepherds is continued by Richard Bellings, a Dubliner, and bears the signature of its native Irish owner, one of the Kennedy clan of the midlands. British and Irish nobility on the banks of the river Liffey shared in the activities and pursuits of their peers in London and in other urban centers across continental Europe.

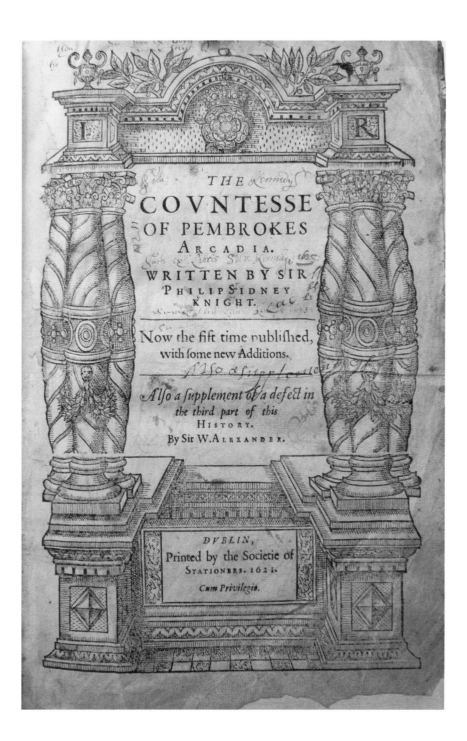

FIGURE 13.7 Sir Philip Sidney (1544–86). *The Countess of Pembrokes Arcadia* (Dublin: Society of Stationers, 1621), title page. Courtesy of Rolf and Magda Loeber.

101

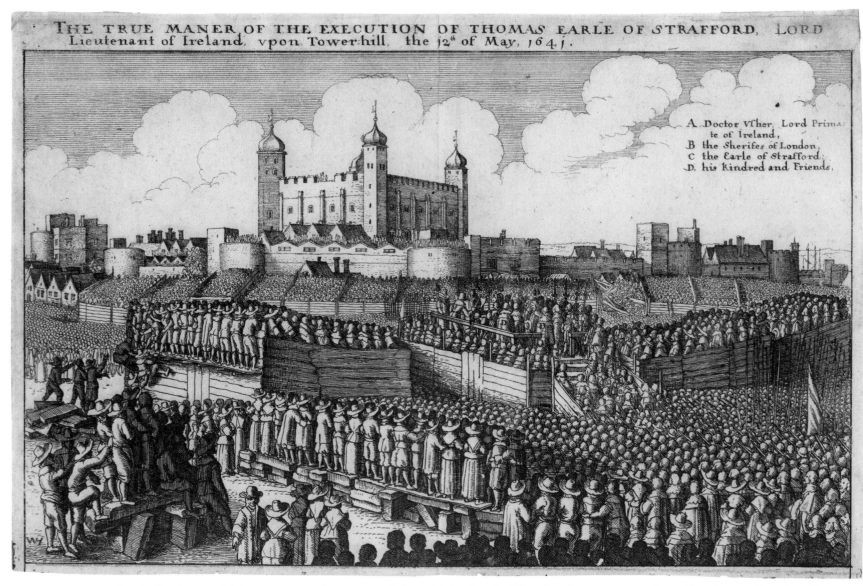

THE TRUE MANER OF THE EXECUTION OF THOMAS EARLE OF STRAFFORD, LORD
Lieutenant of Ireland, vpon Tower-hill, the 12ᵗʰ of May, 1641.

A Doctor Vſher, Lord Prima=
te of Ireland,
B the Sherifes of London,
C the Earle of Strafford,
D his kindred and Friends.

FIGURE 14.1 Wenceslaus Hollar (1607–77) *The true maner of the execution of Thomas Earle of Strafford* ([London, between 1641 and 1677]). Folger Shelf Mark ART 264809.

14
IRISh LONDON, C. 1603-41

THE LONDON OF THE EARLY STUARTS was truly an imperial center. Henry VIII may have made Ireland a kingdom, but James I and his son Charles I governed over all three realms (England, Ireland, and Scotland) and, thus, over a budding British Empire. The imperial crown demanded religious and cultural uniformity of the entire population, not simply the fealty of the elites. Consequently, it had to defend the legitimacy of its claims to Ireland on ideological as well as political grounds. Irish religious, political, social, and economic tensions rocked the court in return.

In response to continued religious controversy, James Ussher, Protestant Archbishop of Armagh and Primate of Ireland, wrote his *Discourse of the Religion Anciently Professed by the Irish and Brittish* (London, 1631; fig. 14.2). In essence, Ussher claimed the Irish religious past for the state-sponsored Protestant church in much the same way that Sir James Ware made a grab for its literary and cultural traditions (see page 97). Ussher knew it was not enough to impose a church on the Irish populace; rather, it had to be demonstrated as natural and historical. Thus, he made the claims that Rome was the real interloper and that the ancient Irish were also sympathetic to the religion brought to them from "Britain" by St. Patrick.

Ussher engaged directly with contemporary religious politics, referring, for example, to O'Sullivan Beare's and Tyrone's treasons and labeling them dupes of a foreign and corrupting "Romish" religion.[54] Instead, history was on his and the state's side. "[A]ll the princes of Ireland" had willingly submitted to the English crown in Henry II's time, and their descendants understood that religious obedience followed

political conformity.[55] By this reasoning, O'Neill et al. were aberrations in their disloyalty, and happily most of "our Nobility and Gentry, by the faithfull service which at that time they performed unto the Crowne of England, did make a real confutation of" claims for a Catholic realm.[56] In the mind of the archbishop, there was a role for the nobility as defenders of the "church by law established," the Protestant Church of Ireland.

In response to the wars raging in all three kingdoms during the 1640s, another staunch anti-Catholic, John Milton, published his *Articles of Peace, Made and Concluded with the Irish Rebels, and Papists . . .*

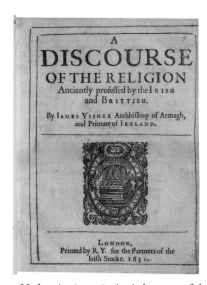

FIGURE 14.2 James Ussher (1581–1656). *A discourse of the religion Anciently professed by the Irish and Brittish* (London: Robert Young, 1631), title page. Folger Shelf Mark STC 24549 copy 1.

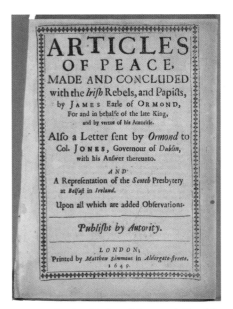

FIGURE 14.3 James Butler, Duke of Ormond, Lord Lieutenant of Ireland, 1649–50. "Observations" attributed to John Milton (1608–74). *Articles of peace, made and concluded with the Irish Rebels, and Papists* (London: Matthew Simmons, 1649), title page. Folger Shelf Mark A3863.

(1649; fig. 14.3). According to Milton, letters intercepted between the twelfth Earl of Ormond and Charles I (reprinted in the work) laid bare royalist conspiracies that threatened to undermine England as a secure and Protestant nation. Charles would be executed that year and the earl fled to the Continent, only to return as Duke of Ormond with the Restoration in 1660. Milton, the political loser at that point, turned to writing *Paradise Lost* in his retirement.

One of the first major casualties of the civil wars was none other than Thomas Wentworth, recently ennobled as the Earl of Strafford. Wentworth had virtually begged his king for a noble title during his tenure as Lord Deputy, the expectation being that were he an earl, many of his opponents in Ireland—both English and Irish—would not be so bold in their insolence. Charles eventually (in 1640) bestowed on him the title Earl of Strafford. His elevation backfired,

however, as Strafford came to be feared as the quintessential "overmighty noble." He was already thought to be an absolutist and to rule with an iron fist; the addition of an aristocratic title served only to make him more menacing.

Complaints of Black Tom Tyrant—as he was called by English and Irish enemies alike—running roughshod over the nobility poured into court. The mailed glove of the state combined with political and religious reform had successfully brought down the Gaelic Irish and Catholic Old English, but Wentworth was also antagonizing the New English magnates, among them Sir John King and Richard Boyle, the first Earl of Cork. Matters came to a head in 1639, after the Scots marched on England, the opening salvo of the wars that shook all three kingdoms. King Charles needed money and he needed arms, and it was feared that Strafford would use his base in Ireland as a launching pad from which to "invade" England with Catholic troops in order to suppress King Charles's parliamentary as well as his Scottish enemies. Impeached and found guilty of treason in the English Parliament and abandoned by his king as a bargaining chip with the House of Commons, Strafford went to his death before a massive crowd eager to see the end of this "noble" enemy of the people (see fig. 14.1).

London's literary scene focused on Ireland and reflected these divisions. John Ford's drama *The Chronicle Historie of Perkin Warbeck* (1634; fig. 14.4) foreshadows the possibility of an Irish-abetted invasion of England led by Strafford: It replayed in London the history of Warbeck's challenge to the English throne at the head of an armed host whose power base lay partly in Ireland (see pages 5 and 7).

But the Irish and the English in Ireland did not want just to invade England; they wanted to enjoy it as well. Like any other imperial center, London proved a great attraction to visiting provincials, including the Irish nobility. The earls of Thomond, for example, spent much of their time in the capital and purchased an estate in Great Billing, Northamptonshire, not far outside the city. Their patronage, in turn,

(*above left*) FIGURE 14.4 John Ford (1586–c. 1640). *The chronicle historie of Perkin Warbeck* (London: Thomas Purfoot, 1634), title page. Folger Shelf Mark STC 11157.

(*above right*) FIGURE 14.5 Owen Felltham (1602?–68). *Resolves: divine, morall, politicall* (London: [Anne Seile], 1661), A1r. Folger Shelf Mark F655.

would contribute much to contemporary intellectual and religious life. For instance, Owen Felltham, author of the popular *Resolves: Divine, Morall, Politicall* (1661; fig. 14.5), a series of short moral lessons for personal improvement, was steward of the family's Northamptonshire estate. Felltham was dedicated to the Stuarts and to the Church of England. Under Cromwell, when the Anglican Book of Common Prayer was banned, Felltham wrote out his own version of the liturgy for use in the Thomond household and dedicated the work to the countess Mary, widow of the fifth earl.[57]

The allure of London society was increasingly felt among Gaelic literati as well. The Kerry poet Piarais Feiritéir penned a love poem (c. 1630s), "Tugas annsacht d'óig Gallda" (I gave my love to a foreign maiden), to Meg Russell, a member of the extended family of the

FIGURE 14.6 Circle of Peter Lely (British, 1618–80). Margaret Russell with her niece Lady Diana (17th century). Reproduced by kind permission of His Grace the Duke of Bedford and the Trustees of the Bedford Estates.

powerful dukes of Bedford (fig. 14.6). She is explicitly referred to as a "Londan-bhean" (London woman) in an example of cross-cultural intoxication and political intrigue (see fig. 14.7):

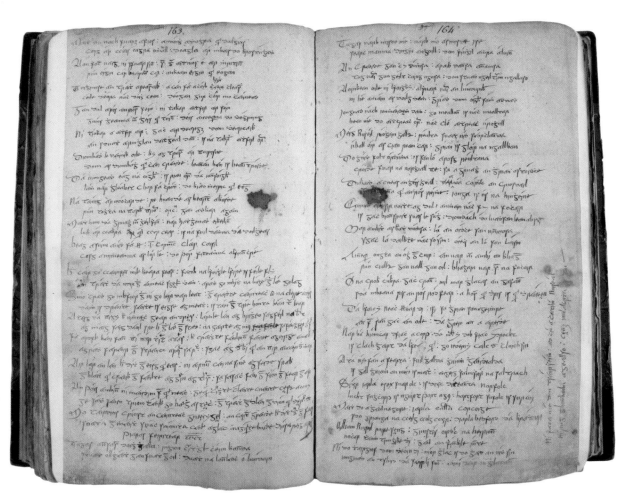

106

FIGURE 14.7
Mícheál Ó Longáin
(1766–1837).
[manuscript], 18th
century, 163–64:
Poem to Meg Russell.
Courtesy of the Royal
Irish Academy, Shelf
Mark MS 23 G 20.

Aoinbhean eile ní bhfuighbheadh,	Any other woman would not receive,
A n-uair uaim an Londain-bhean,	What this London woman got from me,
Ní hé amháin is doiligh dhamh,	Not only is this troubling
Grádh dom oighidh 's dom adhnadh.	But love is destroying and consuming me.
Siúr Iarla Essex fuair uilc,	Her relations are the Earl of Essex, whom harm befell,
Is diuic dícheannta an ór-fhuilt,	And the golden-haired duke who was beheaded,
Lucht sugh-chorp is ngairt-phort ngnaoi,	People of strong bodies and delightful mansions,
Hairfort Sufolc is Suraoi.[58]	Of Hartford, Suffolk and Surrey.[59]

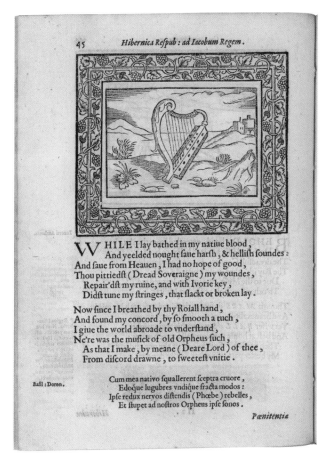

FIGURE 14.8 Henry Peacham (1576?–1643?). *Minerva Britannia, or, A garden of heroical devises* (London: Wa. Dight, [1612]), 45. Folger Shelf Mark STC 19511 copy 1.

FIGURE 14.9 James Howell (1594?–1666). *Mercurius Hibernicus* (Bristol, 1644), sig. A1r. Folger Shelf Mark H3093 Bd.w. STC 7434 copy 2.

We close our catalog with an image of the harp, which was made the national symbol of Ireland not by the Irish but rather by King Henry VIII, who placed it on his coat of arms and on the coin of the realm. Fittingly, the symbol was manipulated for loyalist and rebellious purposes thereafter. Henry Peacham's *Minerva Britannia, or, A Garden of Heroical Devises* (London 1612; fig. 14.8) likens the country's new-found political harmony to the euphonious sound of a harp well tuned by successive English monarchs. An Old English–authored pamphlet of the 1640s, however, depicts a curiously drawn harp as a sign of increased Irish autonomy in turbulent times (fig. 14.9). The marginalia remark how the pamphlet answers Parliamentary lies about the king and the conduct of his forces in Ireland. For both author and reader, a more independent Ireland meant an Ireland under royal rule. In the pamphlet, we see glimpses of the complexity of Ireland's past and future.

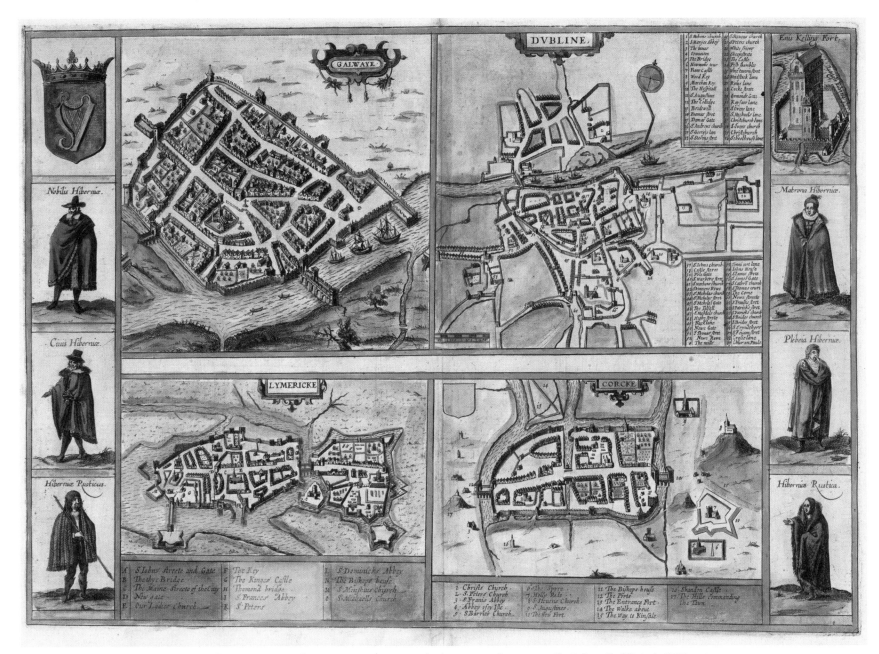

Civitates Orbis Terrarum ([Cologne: Anton Hierat & Abraham Hogenberg, 1618?]). Folger Shelf Mark ART 229985.

EPILOGUE:
CROMWELL, CIVIL WAR, AND RESTORATION,
C. 1641–60

War would come to Ireland in 1641. It began as a noble revolt, not a struggle for national determination. The chief conspirator, Sir Phelim O'Neill, was the head of the O'Neill dynasty. As his knighthood suggests, he was closely aligned with the government of Charles I. Indeed, he owned land in the Ulster Plantation—territory taken from earlier O'Neill lords—and had expelled Gaelic tenants from his lands. He was no simple "faith and fatherland" warrior, but rather another example of the intricate English–Irish interconnections so clearly manifest in the lives of the nobility.

Joining him in rebellion was one of the O'Mores, a noble family who in the 1550s had been run off their traditional lands to make way for the Laois-Offaly plantation scheme. Like his confederate O'Neill, Rory O'More was an Ulster landowner and involved in local politics and society. Their rising was in keeping with the tradition of the "loyal rebellion": an armed demonstration not against the monarch but instead against reputed "evil councilors" who blinded the king's eyes to the loyalty, power, and place of his "true" subjects. Their goal was not to overturn government but rather to improve their place within it. These were men who thought of themselves as noble of birth and deserving of local authority, and they resented being overtaken by those whom they considered upstarts.

Although this exhibition has demonstrated numerous ways in which nobles embodied links and interactions across the Irish Sea, we must remember that nobility also offered a language of resistance. Like Hugh O'Neill and the Earl of Desmond before them, Phelim O'Neill and Rory O'More accused the crown of favoring the lesser born: an inversion of the natural order not to be tolerated.

Unfortunately for these two loyal rebels—and for Ireland—they could not control the forces their actions unleashed. Whatever their "noble" intentions, others used the offensive as cover under which to expel neighboring newcomers who had arrived with the Ulster Plantation. Elite rebellion quickly turned to popular revolt, with many casualties and much loss of property.

Ironically, it would be the English Commons that engineered the destruction of this latest noble rebellion. Propagandists spread tales of the massacre of British settlers, preachers and polemicists called for a holy war of revenge, and Parliament (by means of the Adventurers' Act) facilitated the raising of private support for the war effort by promising the spoils of confiscated Irish lands. English men and money poured once again into battle on Irish shores.

This was no simple conflict of English vs. Irish, however. The Old English, who had resisted Hugh O'Neill's calls for solidarity during the Nine Years' War (1594–1603), joined this rebellion begun by their Gaelic countrymen and, in so doing, ushered in a new chapter in the relations among Irish nobles of different ethnic backgrounds and identities. Together they would proclaim Ireland an independent state and form a government that met in the ancient Ormond stronghold of

Kilkenny. Conspicuously absent from this newly sovereign regime was none other than the current Earl of Ormond, James Butler. Raised as a ward of the English court, the Protestant earl remained loyal to his king and led crown forces in his homeland. Much of the 1640s would be taken up with ancient nobles such as O'Neill and Ormond negotiating truces between "Confederate" and loyalist forces.

Both would lose to commoners in the end. Oliver Cromwell, General of Parliamentary forces and a puritanical critic of class distinctions, arrived in Ireland in 1649. Fresh from defeating royalist forces in England, he brought his lethal mix of military genius and millenarian fury to the western realm. He would spend nine months there, and his armies' victories in a series of ferocious engagements—most notably the sieges-turned-massacres at Drogheda and Wexford—broke the back of Irish resistance. While subordinates mopped up, Cromwell returned to London to rule as king in all but name.

Neither kingdom nor independent state, Ireland in the 1650s would be part of the Commonwealth, a republic under the rule of the Protector and his Parliament. As went the Kingdom of Ireland, so went its nobility. The Cromwellian regime engineered the real revolution of the age: the transfer of land from Catholics to Protestants, many of them soldiers and adventurers, which would forever change the face of Irish society, culture, and politics. (It is estimated that Catholics owned less than ten percent of Irish land by the end of the Interregnum, in 1660.)

Vincent Gookin promoted efforts at seeing the Irish commons remain on the land and the nobility and gentry dispossessed. In his pamphlet *The Great Case of Transplantation in Ireland Discussed,*[60] he championed the cause of the laboring Irish who lived and worked alongside English settlers and under English masters. The nobles, by contrast, were welcome—as Cromwell is famously alleged to have said—to go to "hell or Connacht." Nevertheless, Gookin felt that the Irish would make loyal and productive subjects. A patronizing colonialist though

he may have been, Gookin at least disavowed the aggressive solutions promoted by hard-line theorists such as Edmund Spenser.

Many of those who fought for King or Confederacy went overseas. Ormond, for example, joined the King's son—the putative Charles II—in exile in France. Those left at home savagely critiqued their new governors. Ireland had become overrun with "clownish upstarts" and "fat-rumped jeerers . . . with shaven jaws, English talk and braggart accent," complained the poet Dáibhídh Ó Bruadair in 1652.[61] As he saw things, the only ones to prosper in the new Ireland were the aggressive, the uneducated, and the heretical. Not only had his noble patrons disappeared; so too had nobility itself. The triumph of Parliament seemed to ring the death knell of aristocratic influence in Irish affairs, even while it helped drive exiled Irish and English elites closer together in shared horror at the rule of the Commons.

The 1660s, then, must have seemed miraculous. With the restoration of Charles II to his triple crown in 1660, the nobility once again came to dominate Irish politics and society. If anything, they were even more closely connected to the English court than were their pre-1641 predecessors. Indeed, the year 1661 witnessed a phenomenon not seen since the 1530s: the naming of an Irish-born nobleman (Ormond) as Lord Lieutenant of the kingdom. Dublin once again would hum to the rhythms of the elite "seasons" as nobles flocked to the capital city and its metropolitan charms: courts, Parliament, business, theater, music, parlors, duels, races, and the like.

But in two important ways this was a new age from that of the 1530s. First, Gaelic nobles were no longer players on the great stage of "British" politics. Gone were the days when O'Neills and McCarthys commanded the attention of crown and Parliament. The Irish language was in decline, the bards a thing of the past, and the great dynasties increasingly the subject of nostalgia. Second, Catholic nobles were largely absent from the corridors of real power. King Charles II's brother, James II, would make an effort to restore Catholicism to the realms. His Lord Deputy, Richard Talbot Earl of Tyrconnell, was an Irish-born noble of Old English stock and a Catholic. The invasion of the Protestant William of Orange, however, would end their revolution. The final showdown took place on Irish soil as William's forces routed James's in battles from the Boyne in the east to Aughrim in the west.

Visitors to present-day Dublin are immediately aware of the influence of the nobility in Ireland, which lasted well past the so-called Glorious Revolution. The city's unrivaled Georgian splendor speaks to its emergence in the eighteenth century as the second city of the realms, and art and architecture flourished under the patronage of those who would come to be known as the Ascendancy class. A short trip south of the city to the Wicklow Mountains, however, reminds the traveler that an old nobility descended as the new one rose. There, little remains to be seen of the once mighty O'Byrnes, Gaelic nobles who challenged Elizabeth's Irish government in the field and fostered art and learning in their mountain courts.

With the Ascendancy, "nobility and newcomers" became increasingly one and the same: Recent arrivals and their descendants, not the old names, filled the heralds' rolls. Free State and early Republic leaders in twentieth-century Ireland would attempt to relegate both to the political sidelines. Their imagined state was Gaelic, mainly Catholic, and populist (if not fully democratic).

Nobility, then, could be a divisive force in English–Irish relations as well as a unifying one. We miss a crucial element in the history of Ireland—indeed of England, Britain, and America too—by overlooking nobles and newcomers in Renaissance Ireland: a history of interaction and interconnection, at some times in conflict and at others cooperative, that helped shape the modern island, its people, and their place in the world.

111

NOTES

INTRODUCTION

1 Understood here as the period 1450–1700: from the time of Richard, the third Duke of York and seventh Earl of Ulster's government in Ireland as Lord Lieutenant; through the Tudor, Stuart, Cromwellian, and Restoration periods; and to the Battle of the Boyne and the "Glorious" Revolution (1690). Among key dates are of Ireland becoming a kingdom under Tudor rule (1541) and of the start of Stuart rule (1603).

2 In the book's sequel, *Scarlett* (1991), by Alexandra Ripley, Scarlett returns to her ancestral Irish home—led there by a Fenian priest, her cousin Colum—and there becomes "Chief of his Name," or "The O'Hara."

3 Remnants of noble families in the Republic were largely dispossessed in the nineteenth and twentieth centuries or absorbed, at least visibly, by the redistribution of wealth and democratic politics following the country's independence from Britain, in 1922. Some of the aristocracy at that point simply left the country. Others left long before that, or died out. Still others stayed, and indeed some of their descendants are in today's Ireland.
    The Irish Constitution of 1937 forbids conferring of noble titles by the state, and in 2003 the practice of official recognition by the state of a "Chief of the Name," or Head of extended family, was also abandoned. For a discussion of the remnants of Irish nobility *in situ* today, see Anne Chambers, *At Arm's Length: Aristocrats in the Republic of Ireland* (Dublin: New Island Books, 2005).

4 A collection of essays on the castle has just appeared: Jane Fenlon, ed., *Clanricard's Castle: Portumna House, Co. Galway* (Dublin: Four Courts Press, 2012).

5 Recently published on this castle are two scholarly books: James Lyttleton, *Blarney Castle: An Irish Tower House* (Dublin: Four Courts Press, 2011); and Mark Samuel and Kate Hamlyn, *Blarney Castle: Its History, Development, and Purpose* (Cork: Cork University Press, 2008).

6 A finely illustrated book about it has followed: Colin Breen, *Dunluce Castle: History and Archaeology* (Dublin: Four Courts Press, 2012).

7 Elizabeth FitzPatrick, *Royal Inauguration in Gaelic Ireland, c. 1100–1600: A Cultural Landscape Study* (Suffolk, UK: Boydell Press, 2004).

8 In the early-modern period, Devonshire supplied many English colonists to Ireland, among them Sir Walter Raleigh.

9 Manus O'Donnell, *The Life of Colum Cille,* Brian Lacey, ed. and trans. (Dublin: Four Courts Press, 1998).

10 Recent trends in Irish historiography stress the suffering caused by warfare in particular. See, for example, David Edwards, *Age of Atrocity: Violence and Political Conflict in Early Modern Ireland,* Pádraig Lenihan and Clodagh Tait, eds. (Dublin: Four Courts Press, 2007).

11 The poem "Cnoc Samhraidh" appears in: Pádraig de Brún, Breandán Ó Buachalla, and Tomás Ó Concheanainn, *Nua-dhuanaire I* (Dublin: Dublin Institute for Advanced Studies; 1971, reprint 1997), 7–8.

CHAPTER 1

12 William Shakespeare, *Second Part of Henry the Sixth* (New York: Washington Square Press [1966]), act 5, sc. 1, lines 1–4. Folger Shelf Mark PR2753 .W8 1959 v.13.

13 Great Britain. Office of the Revels. Revells ffrom shrovetide. Manuscript (1554–55), leaf 2v. Folger Shelf Mark L.b.302.

CHAPTER 2

14 The Folger copy is the only one in North America. No illustrations remain in it, and most other surviving copies have few or none. The only complete set of illustrations is found in the copy held at the library of the University of Edinburgh. Folger Shelf Mark STC 6734.

15 John Derricke, *The Image of Irelande with a Discoverie of Wood Karne* (1581), edited by D. B. Quinn (Belfast: Blackstaff Press, 1985), 68.

16 Lodowick Bryskett, *A Discourse of civill life* (London: William Aspley, 1606), 117–18. Folger Shelf Mark STC 3959.

17 *The famous historye of the life and death of Captaine Thomas Stukeley* ([London]: [William Jaggard], 1605), 40. Folger Shelf Mark STC 23405 copy 2.

CHAPTER 3

18 Virgil, *The first foure bookes of Virgils Aeneis,* Richard Stanyhurst, trans. (London: Henrie Bynneman, 1583), A8r. Folger Shelf Mark STC 24807.

19 *Songes and sonets written by the right honorable Lorde Henry Haward late Earle of Surrey* ([London]: Richard Tottell, 1574), fol. 5r. Folger Shelf Mark STC 13866 copy 1.

CHAPTER 4

20 Dermot O'Meara, *Ormonius* (London: Thomas Snodham, 1615), Folger Shelf Mark STC 17761.

21 David Edwards and Keith Sidwell, eds., *The Tipperary Hero: Dermot O'Meara's "Ormonius,"* (Turnhout, Belgium, and Washington, DC: Brepols, 2012).

22 J. O'Daly (trans.), "Panegyric on Thomas Butler, the 10th earl of Ormonde," *Transactions of the Kilkenny Archaeological Society* 1 (1849–51), 474–75.

23 Edmund Spenser, *The faerie queene* (London: [John Wolfe], 1590), 2Q2v. Folger Shelf Mark STC 23080.

CHAPTER 5

24 James Carney, ed. and trans., *Medieval Irish Lyrics* (Dublin: Dolmen Press, 1967), 92–93.

25 Edmund Spenser, *View of the present state of Ireland*, W. L. Renwick, ed. (London: E. Partridge, at the Scholartis Press, 1934).

26 Ibid., *The faerie queene* (London: [Richard Field], 1596), Book 3, verses 20–22. Folger Shelf Mark STC 23082 copy 2.

chapter 6

27 Despite tradition that the sitter of this well-known portrait is Spenser, his identity is unknown.

28 Edmund Spenser, *Colin Clouts come home againe* (London: T[homas] C[reede], 1595). Folger Shelf Mark STC 23077 copy 4.

29 Lodowick Bryskett, "A Pastoral Aeglogue upon the Death of Sir Phillip Sidney Knight, etc.," *Colin Clouts come home againe,* Edmund Spenser (London, 1595), H2r.

30 Identified by the writer Colm Tóibín as the Urrin, in Enniscorthy, County Wexford, Bryskett's adopted town in Leinster.

31 Osborn Bergin, *Irish Bardic Poetry: Text and translations together with an introductory lecture* (Dublin: Dublin Institute for Advanced Studies, 1970), 125–26.

32 Thomas Kinsella, ed. and trans., *The New Oxford Book of Irish Verse* (Oxford and New York: Oxford University Press, 1986), 160–61.

chapter 7

33 Sir John Davies, *Historical relations: or, a discovery of the true causes why Ireland was never entirely subdued nor brought under obedience of the crown of England* (Dublin, 1664). Folger Shelf Mark D401.

34 Lambert McKenna, ed. and trans., *Aithdioghluim Dána,* vol. 40 of *Irish Texts Society Series,* part I (Dublin: Educational Co. of Ireland, 1939–40), 107.

35 Ibid., part II, 64.

36 Conrad Heresbach, *Foure Bookes of Husbandry* (London: [John Kingston], 1587), (ij)r. Folger Shelf Mark STC 13197 copy 2.

chapter 8

37 Bagot Papers. Letter from Robert Bagot to Richard Bagot (Dublin: 1587–88). Folger Shelf Mark L.a.85.

38 William Shakespeare, *The Life of Henry V,* eds. Barbara A. Mowat and Paul Werstine (New York: Washington Square Press, 1995), act 5, lines 23–35. Folger Shelf Mark PR2753 .M6 2003 copy 2 v.11.

chapter 9

39 Lambert McKenna, ed. and trans., *Aithdioghluim Dána,* 2 vols. (Dublin 1939, 1940); v.1, 179.

40 Ibid., v.2, 105.

41 Ben Jonson, "The Irish Masque at Court" in *The Workes of Benjamin Jonson* (London, 1616), 1003–4.

42 Historical extracts, c. 1625. Manuscript, leaf 24r. Folger Shelf Mark X.d.393.

chapter 10

43 Eleanor Knott, ed. and trans., "The Flight of the Earls 1607," in *Ériu* 8 (Dublin: Royal Irish Academy, 1916), 192.

44 Ibid., 193.

45 Tadhg O Cianáin, *Turas na dTaoiseach nUltach as Éirinn* (Rome: Pontifical Irish College, 2007), 87. Folger Shelf Mark D915 .O313 2007.

46 Ibid., 293.

chapter 11

47 William Shakespeare, *The Tempest* (New York: Washington Square Press, 1961), act 2, sc. 1, lines 157–60. Folger Shelf Mark PR2753 .W8 1959 v.31.

48 Sir John Davies, *A discoverie of the true causes why Ireland was never entirely Subdued* (London: [William Jaggard], 1612), 272. Folger Shelf Mark STC 6348.

49 Shakespeare, *The Tempest,* act 2, sc. 1, lines 175–80.

chapter 12

50 Letter from Sir Thomas Pope to Sir William Pope (October 10, 1628). Manuscript, fol. 115. Oxford University, Bodleian Library, North MS C. 7.

51 John Cusack, *Ireland's Comfort* (Ireland, 1629?), 174v. Folger Shelf Mark G.a.10.

chapter 13

52 Edmund Spenser, *A view of the [present] state of Ireland* in Edmund Campion, *Two histories of Ireland* (Dublin: Society of Stationers, 1633), 173. Folger Shelf Mark STC 25067a copy 2.

53 James Shirley, *St. Patrick for Ireland* (London: I. Raworth, 1640). Folger Shelf Mark STC 22455 copy 1.

chapter 14

54 James Ussher, *A discourse of the religion Anciently professed by the Irish and Brittish* (London: R[obert] Y[oung], 1631), 123, 128.

55 Ibid., 118.

56 Ibid., 130. Folger Shelf Mark STC 24549 copy 1, 118, 123, 138, 131.

57 Owen Felltham (1602?–68), *Resolves: divine, morall, politicall* (London: [Anne Seile], 1661), A1r. Folger Shelf Mark F655.

58 Pat Muldowney, ed. and trans., *Dánta P[h]iarais Feiritéir* (Aubane, Cork: Aubane Historical Society, 1999), 56, 60.

59 Ibid., 57, 61.

epilogue

60 Vincent Gookin (1616?–1659), *The great case of transplantation in Ireland discussed* (London: for John Crook, 1655). Folger Shelf Mark G1274.

61 John C. MacErlean, ed. and trans. *Duanaire D[h]áib[h]id[h] Uí B[h]ruadair: The Poems of David Ó Bruadair,* part I (Dublin, Irish Texts Society), 37.

BIBLIOGRAPHY

Asch, Ronald. *Nobilities in Transition 1550–1700: Courtiers and Rebels in Britain and Europe*. New York: Arnold, 2003.

Barnard, Toby. *Making the Grand Figure: Lives and Possession in Ireland, 1641–1770*. New Haven: Yale University Press, 2004.

Barnard, Toby, and Jane Fenlon, eds. *The Dukes of Ormond, 1610–1745*. Woodbridge, Suffolk, UK: Boydell Press, 2000.

Barton, D. Plunket. *Links Between Ireland and Shakespeare*. Dublin: Talbot Press, 1919.

Berleth, Richard. *The Twilight Lords: An Irish Chronicle*. New York: Viking, 1978.

Braddick, Michael. *State Formation in Early Modern England, c. 1550–1700*. Cambridge: Cambridge University Press, 2000.

Braddick, Michael, and John Walter, eds. *Negotiating Power in Early Modern Society: Order, Hierarchy and Subordination in Britain and Ireland*. Cambridge: Cambridge University Press, 2001.

Bradshaw, Brendan. *The Irish Constitutional Revolution of the Sixteenth Century*. Cambridge: Cambridge University Press, 1979.

Bradshaw, Brendan, Andrew Hadfield, and Willy Maley, eds. *Representing Ireland: Literature and the Origins of Conflict, 1534–1660*. Cambridge: Cambridge University Press, 1993.

Bradshaw, Brendan, and John Morrill, eds. *The British Problem, c. 1534–1707: State Formation in the Atlantic Archipelago*. New York: Palgrave Macmillan, 1996.

Brady, Ciaran. *The Chief Governors: The Rise and Fall of Reform Government in Tudor Ireland, 1536–88*. Cambridge: Cambridge University Press, 1994.

———. *Shane O'Neill*. Dundalk: Dundalgan Press, 1996.

Brady, Ciaran, and Raymond Gillespie, eds. *Natives and Newcomers: The Making of Irish Colonial Society, 1534–1641*. Dublin: Irish Academic Press, 1986.

Breatneach, Pádraig A. "The Chief's Poet." *Proceedings of the Royal Irish Academy* 83c (1983), 37–79.

———. *Téamaí taighde Nua-Ghaeilge*. Dublin: An Sagart, 1997.

Breen, Colin. *Dunluce Castle: History and Archaeology*. Dublin: Four Courts Press, 2012.

Burnett, Mark Thornton, and Ramona Wray, eds. *Shakespeare and Ireland: History, Politics, Culture*. New York: St. Martin's Press, 1997.

Byrne, Francis J. *Irish Kings and High-Kings*. London: B. T. Batsford, 1973.

Caball, Marc. *Poets and Politics: Continuity and Reaction in Irish Poetry, 1558–1625*. South Bend, Indiana: University of Notre Dame Press, 1999.

Canny, Nicholas. *Making Ireland British, 1580–1650*. New York: Oxford University Press, 2001.

———. *The Upstart Earl: A Study of the Social and Mental World of Richard Boyle, First Earl of Cork, 1566–1643*. Cambridge: Cambridge University Press, 1982.

Carey, Vincent. *Surviving the Tudors: The Wizard Earl of Kildare and English Rule in Ireland, 1537–1586*. Dublin: Four Courts Press, 2002.

Carney, James. *The Irish Bardic Poet*. Dublin: The Dolmen Press, 1967.

Chambers, Anne. *As Wicked a Woman: Eleanor, Countess of Desmond*. Dublin: Wolfhound Press, 1986.

———. *At Arm's Length: Aristocrats in the Republic of Ireland*. Dublin: New Island, 2004.

———. *Granuaile: The Life and Times of Grace O'Malley, c. 1530–1603*. Dublin: Wolfhound Press, 1979; rev. ed. 1998.

———. *Shadow Lord: Theobald Burke, Tibbot-ne-Long, 1567–1629: Son of the Pirate Queen, Grace O'Malley*. Dublin: Ashfield Press, 2007.

Clark, Peter, and Raymond Gillespie, eds. *Two Capitals: London and Dublin, 1500–1840*. Oxford: The British Academy and Oxford University Press, 2001.

Clarke, Aidan. *The Old English in Ireland, 1625–42*. Reprint edition. Dublin: Four Courts Press, 2000.

Derricke, John. *The Image of Irelande* (1581). Ed. D. B. Quinn. Belfast: Blackstaff Press, 1985.

Doran, Linda, and James Lyttleton, eds. *Lordship in Medieval Ireland: Image and Reality*. Dublin: Four Courts Press, 2008.

Edwards, David. *The Ormond Lordship in County Kilkenny, 1515–1642. The Rise and Fall of Butler Feudal Power.* Dublin: Four Courts Press, 2003.

———, ed. *Regions and Rulers in Ireland, 1100–1650.* Dublin: Four Courts Press, 2004.

Edwards, David, Pádraig Lenihan, and Clodagh Tait, eds. *Age of Atrocity: Violence and Political Conflict in Early Modern Ireland.* Dublin: Four Courts Press, 2007.

Ellis, Steven. *Tudor Frontiers and Noble Power: The Making of the British State.* Oxford: Oxford University Press, 1995.

Fenlon, Jane, ed. *Clanricard's Castle: Portumna House, Co. Galway.* Dublin: Four Courts Press, 2012.

FitzPatrick, Elizabeth. *Royal Inauguration in Gaelic Ireland, c. 1100–1600: A Cultural Landscape Study.* Woodbridge, Suffolk, UK: Boydell Press, 2004.

Fletcher, Alan. *Drama, Performance and Polity in Pre-Cromwellian Ireland.* Toronto: University of Toronto Press, 2000.

Gillespie, Raymond. *Colonial Ulster: The Settlement of East Ulster, 1600–1641.* Cork: Irish Committee of Historical Sciences, 1985.

———. *Seventeenth-Century Ireland: Making Ireland Modern.* Dublin: Gill and Macmillan, 2006.

Hadfield, Andrew. *Edmund Spenser: A Life.* Oxford, UK: Oxford University Press, 2012.

———. *Spenser's Irish Experience: Wilde Fruit and Salvage Soyl.* Oxford: Oxford University Press, 1997.

Hamilton, A. C., ed. *The Spenser Encyclopedia.* Toronto: University of Toronto Press, 1990.

Hammer, Paul. *The Polarisation of Elizabethan Politics: The Political Career of Robert Devereux, 2nd Earl of Essex, 1585–1597.* Cambridge: Cambridge University Press, 1999.

Herron, Thomas. *Spenser's Irish Work: Poetry, Plantation and Colonial Reformation.* Aldershot, UK: Ashgate, 2007.

Herron, Thomas, and Willy Maley, eds. *Sir Henry Sidney in Ireland and Wales. Sidney Journal* 29.1–2 (2011).

Herron, Thomas, and Michael Potterton, eds. *Ireland in the Renaissance, c. 1540–1660.* Dublin: Four Courts Press, 2007.

Kane, Brendan. *The Politics and Culture of Honour in Britain and Ireland, 1541–1641.* Cambridge: Cambridge University Press, 2010.

Leerssen, Joep. *Mere Irish and Fíor-Ghael: Studies in the Idea of Irish Nationality, Its Development and Literary Expression prior to the Nineteenth Century.* South Bend, IN: University of Notre Dame Press, 1986.

Lennon, Colm. *The Lords of Dublin in an Age of Reformation.* Dublin: Irish Academic Press, 1989.

———. *Richard Stanihurst the Dubliner, 1547–1618.* Dublin: Irish Academic Press, 1981.

———. *Sixteenth-Century Ireland: The Incomplete Conquest.* Rev. ed. Dublin: Gill and Macmillan, 2005.

Lyons, Mary Ann, and Thomas O'Connor. *Strangers to Citizens: The Irish in Europe, 1600–1800.* Dublin: National Library of Ireland, 2008.

Lyttleton, James. *Blarney Castle: An Irish Tower House.* Dublin: Four Courts Press, 2011.

Lyttleton, James, and Colin Rynne, eds. *Plantation Ireland: Settlement and Material Culture, c. 1550–c. 1700.* Dublin: Four Courts Press, 2009.

MacCarthy-Morrogh, Michael. *The Munster Plantation: English Migration to Southern Ireland, 1583–1641.* Oxford: Clarendon Press, 1986.

Maginn, Christopher. *"Civilizing" Gaelic Leinster: The Extension of Tudor Rule in the O'Byrne and O'Toole Lordships.* Dublin: Four Courts Press, 2005.

———. "The Gaelic Peers, the Tudor Sovereigns, and English Multiple Monarchy." *The Journal of British Studies* 50, 3 (2011), 566–86.

Maley, Willy. *Salvaging Spenser: Colonialism, Culture and Identity.* London: Palgrave Macmillan, 1997.

Mayes, Charles. "The Early Stuarts and the Irish Peerage." *English Historical Review* 73, 287 (1958), 227–51.

———. "The Sale of Peerages in Early Stuart England." *The Journal of Modern History* 29, 1 (1957), 21–37.

McCabe, Richard. *Spenser's Monstrous Regiment: Elizabethan Ireland and the Poetics of Difference.* Oxford: Oxford University Press, 2002.

McCormack, Anthony. *The Earldom of Desmond, 1463–1583: The Decline and Crisis of a Feudal Lordship.* Dublin: Four Courts Press, 2005.

McCorristine, Laurence. *The Revolt of Silken Thomas: A Challenge to Henry VIII.* Dublin: Wolfhound Press, 1987.

McGowan-Doyle, Valerie. *The Book of Howth: Elizabethan Conquest and the Old English.* Cork: University of Cork Press, 2011.

McGuire, J. J., ed. *Dictionary of Irish Biography.* 9 vols. Cambridge: Cambridge University Press, 2009.

Merritt, J. F., ed. *The Political World of Thomas Wentworth, Earl of Strafford, 1621–1641.* Cambridge: Cambridge University Press, 2003.

Mhac an tSaoi, Máire. *Cérbh í Meg Russell? Dearcadh as Shaolré Phiarais Fheiritéir agus go háirithe ar an bpáirt inti a bhí ag Richard Boyle, Iarla Chorcaí.* Galway: Leabhar Breac, 2008.

Moody, T. W., et al. (eds.). *A New History of Ireland,* vol. 3: *Early Modern Ireland, 1534–1691.* Oxford: Oxford University Press, 1986.

Morgan, Hiram. *Tyrone's Rebellion: The Outbreak of the Nine Years' War in Tudor Ireland.* Dublin: Boydell, 1999.

———, ed. *The Battle of Kinsale.* Bray, Ireland: Wordwell, 2004.

———. *Political Ideology in Ireland, 1541–1641.* Dublin: Four Courts Press, 1999.

Murray, Peter, ed. *Portraits and People: Art in Seventeenth-Century Ireland.* Cork: Crawford Art Gallery, 2010.

O'Brien, Conor, ed. *Feagh McHugh O'Byrne: The Wicklow Firebrand, a Volume of Quatercentennial Essays. Journal of the Rathdrum Historical Society* I (1998).

Ó Buachalla, Breandán. *Aisling Ghéar: Na Stíobhartaigh agus an tAos Léinn, 1603–1778.* Dublin: An Clóchomhar, 1996.

———. *The Crown of Ireland.* Galway: Arlen House, 2006.

———. "James Our True King: The Ideology of Irish Royalism in the Seventeenth Century," in D. G. Boyce, ed. *Political Thought in Ireland Since the Seventeenth Century.* London: Routledge, 1998.

O'Byrne, Emmett. *War, Politics and the Irish of Leinster.* Dublin: Four Courts Press, 2003.

Ó Cuív, Brian. *The Irish Bardic Duanaire or Poem-Book.* Dublin: Malton, 1973.

O'Donnell, Manus. *The Life of Colum Cille* (1534). Ed. and trans. Brian Lacy. Dublin: Four Courts Press, 1998.

Ohlmeyer, Jane. *Making Ireland English: The Irish Aristocracy in the Seventeenth Century.* New Haven: Yale University Press, 2012.

———, ed. *Political Thought in Seventeenth-Century Ireland: Kingdom or Colony?* Cambridge: Cambridge University Press, 2000.

O'Meara, Dermot. *The Tipperary Hero: Dermot O'Meara's "Ormonius"* (1615). Eds. David Edwards and Keith Sidwell. Trans. Keith Sidwell. Turnhout, Belgium: Brepols, 2012.

O'Riordan, Michelle. *The Gaelic Mind and the Collapse of the Gaelic World.* Cork: Cork University Press, 1990.

Ó Siochrú, Mícheál. *God's Executioner: Oliver Cromwell and the Conquest of Ireland.* London: Faber and Faber, 2008.

Palmer, Patricia. *Language and Conquest in Early Modern Ireland: English Renaissance Literature and Elizabethan Imperial Expansion.* Cambridge: Cambridge University Press, 2001.

Pawlisch, Hans. *Sir John Davies and the Conquest of Ireland: A Study in Legal Imperialism.* Cambridge: Cambridge University Press, 1985.

Pope Hennessy, John. *Sir Walter Raleigh in Ireland* (1883). Ed. Thomas Herron. Dublin: University College Press, 2009.

Potterton, Michael, and Thomas Herron, eds. *Dublin and the Pale in the Renaissance, c. 1540–1660.* Dublin: Four Courts Press, 2012.

Power, Gerald. *A European Frontier Elite: The Nobility of the English Pale in Tudor Ireland, 1496–1566.* Hanover, Germany: Wehrhahn Verlag, 2012.

Quinn, David Beers. *The Elizabethans and the Irish.* Ithaca, New York: The Folger Library and Cornell University Press, 1966.

Samuel, Mark, and Kate Hamlyn. *Blarney Castle: Its History, Development and Purpose.* Cork: Cork University Press, 2008.

Simms, Katherine. *From Kings to Warlords: The Changing Political Structure of Gaelic Ireland in the Later Middle Ages.* Dublin: Boydell, 2000.

Stanihurst, Richard. *Aeneis* (1582). Ed. Dirk van der Haar. Amsterdam: H. J. Paris, 1933.

Stone, Lawrence. *The Crisis of the Aristocracy.* Oxford: Oxford University Press, 1971.

Tait, Clodagh. *Death, Burial and Commemoration in Ireland, 1550–1650.* New York: Palgrave Macmillan, 2002.

Treadwell, Victor. *Buckingham and Ireland, 1616–1628: A Study in Anglo-Irish Politics.* Dublin: Four Courts Press, 1998.

Walsh, Micheline Kerney. *An Exile of Ireland: Hugh O'Neill, Prince of Ulster.* Dublin: Four Courts Press, 1996.

Williams, Nicholas. *Armas: Sracfhéacaint ar Araltas na hÉireann.* Dublin: Coiscéim, 2001.

116

A CRÍOCH SIN

THOMAS HERRON is Associate Professor of English at East Carolina University, Greenville, North Carolina, teaching Shakespeare and Renaissance literature. He is the author of *Edmund Spenser's Irish Work: Poetry, Plantation and Colonial Reformation* (2007) as well as co-editor (with Michael Potterton) of both *Ireland and the Renaissance, 1540–1660* (2007) and *Dublin and the Pale in the Renaissance, 1540–1660* (2011). He currently edits the multidisciplinary journal *Explorations in Renaissance Culture.*

BRENDAN KANE is Associate Professor of History at the University of Connecticut and Associate Director of the University of Connecticut Humanities Institute. In addition to teaching broadly in early-modern European history, he offers classes in Irish Gaelic. He is the author of *The Politics and Culture of Honour in Britain and Ireland, 1541–1641* (2010) and co-editor (with Valerie McGowan-Doyle) of a forthcoming collection of essays entitled *Elizabeth I and Ireland.*

The text of this book is composed in Adobe Garamond printing types, designed by Robert Slimbach. They resemble the types used by Irish and English printers in the period with which the catalog and exhibition are concerned. The display type is Karlgeorg Hoefer's Omnia uncial. We are thankful to James Mosley, Pádraig Ó Macháin, and Colin Dunn for their counsel in the selection of the types. Attentively copy edited and proofread by Doris Troy. Printed by Penmor Lithographers on acid-free Cougar text and cover. Smythsewn and bound by Acme Bookbinding for a long reference life. Design and typography by Bruce Kennett, who consumed gallons of Upton's "River Shannon" tea while making the book.

The Gentleman of Ireland   The Gentlewoman of Ireland

The Civill Irish Woman   The Civill Irish man

The Wilde Irish man   The Wilde Irish Woman

Jodocus Hondius celavit

WEST OCEAN

Place names (map):

Coun
Kelban Montaghu M.Lelen Newcastle
C.Donnell Og Lacuath Ben Slew Clunebo Reagh M.Idagh Conogher John Amoy
Can Leame Hoghnis Lyfanyn Atlone
Crogh M.Darra C.Tig Letter Rofrial Earle of Clanricket Clogh Clonbegny
Reil ca Agaro Downe ca Sheney
Scardies C.Nemene Clare Sormore Kellean Barony of Atlone Shug ca More cast
Can Leteman Morklon ca Barony of Killoan
Great Iland Balant court Galway Kirges towne Lackfin Drogh Kilharon Clunes
Serne Gal Barony of Lenyn
S.Greggries found The Bay of S.Bride Marogh Way Millech
Black rock Kilmacullo L.Rea Lackin M.Sy
The Iles of Galway Nelly Leuran Kilroy Coun C.Ke
Arran C.Shaghn Lameuanton
Smale Glaniog ca Inguint B.Berre
S.Sound Corcuna Incherone Syrag Rofcene
Can Braine Phelim Coun C.Mule Mollin
Tomalyn Max The 12 great
Can Calew Clone Ray C Terreda Palace Ilales of Phelim
Leskenny C.Raone Kilmor Clare Killeloe Searroik Ghe.Madona
Enis Kery Killynerock Huyfk Tollogh Coun L.Palace
C.Glame C.Carbely Doun ca Dorles
Moy ca Toamh C.Cleary Type
Done more Donoghan Tomound Agnay Trough ca Clankard
Moore Bay Kellegh Crobraken Claremon Clay cast Triperan Camyk
Downekey Dingan Clare Droncley C.Donell Meyth Canmys
Ket Ca Neregor C.Nono Owin Grenand Kilyhen
Donesanan Belzer Tyke Came Shenni Au Lymericke Lyfkyn Knochord Lysmolkey
Carygoly M.Otton Drombony Romare B.Grand M.Caer
Killaus C.Bay Holon Caergonia L. Gher nan ghedy Roth
Can Leane C.Beale Haguella C.Torbet Longhill Adare M.Galtoni
C.Manyn Afketin Ragha Oghan U
Can Sanan Prof Au C.Gorgrey Coun. Grome Torlboy Santon
Cadon Ballylogan M Torlboy M.Lander
Newtown New Caftle MO
Lyftoule C.Norra Donepatrick
Hogges Mychamy Lixnayo Slew Logher C.Englyh Euloghan Wyftell
Coun: M.Eyrleyson Kilnolan Corre
Bernogh M.Trayle C.Non Arnecragh C.Drynad Ouella
Glan Flyx Caure Rame Nath
CCurny McKylnoglefe Slew pappa Teben C.Catane
Carydone C.Galley C.Gregory Kery C.Wing Count. Derifham Ca Cantorke Ca.Loughurt C.Lynyhro
C.Mores Defmod E.of Lyfter Moor County
Shroe C.Feriter Glan L.Larne Knock Muskery Whitchurch McArmoy Lyons
E.of Dyngle C.Lander Carta Lyf.L.Leyer Horney Mologderre Rahufk Balen M.Malhan
Venoray Dyngle C.Mynet Caherilon Ca.Talace S Corck R.Cormog Killare
Dyngle Bay Ryth M.Caere Donclow Tork Arthully C.Inch Caregha C.Christian
Can des Rylkorbe New Lo. Barnfey Ryteogh Au C.Kulligray Barnella Cariklint Hagha Ado
Cytty Polgoran church Cyty Defmond Flenoker Corck Clone
Can Dolos C.Carbe Ran Mary Done lyrk M.Carta Corbet
Kylyland Polirfdragh Ardey Mayngh Ca.Kylbrytayn Kynfale Trasakin
C.Letter Ardey montaun Clan Dormond Corck haven Caa Dinerum
Valentia Lemgore Mayngh Clangryne Lifferem
Lonmayn Mayre Auxuis Donena M.Tomalegh Kynfale haue Lazolon
Middle Skyl Ivgh Codihead Woday M.Bautry Head of Kynfale
Skyllygh M Kau Letty Carowaarhr Barretes
Can Dolos run Clacauuas Seale Donc ca C.Ray
M.Traghware Slew Mefk Cara O Dtrykall C.Logh
Weris Hoge head Kyrde Grat I Salmon Leape Kilga Can Donedoly
Skryft Incolagh Skyrth Clogh Deloghe
Caribies Loughan Doneboys Baire Au Roftrenno Ogge
Moko lagh Ghedagh Kilmore Eragh C.Cone Perles Stigor
Towne Downlough Lerago ca Castles
Bayle Shepes head Bellemire Au Bord Cryg
Doxfes The Cate Crye
Miffen head Bord R.Gafcon Stokes of Balatimore
Beare borne bay Tolder Baltimore bay Cape Cleare Fastenay

WEST   SO